Teaching Problem-Solving and Thinking Skills through Science

Exciting cross-curricular challenges for foundation phase and key stages one and two

Belle Wallace, Diana Cave and Andrew Berry

Routledge
Taylor & Francis Group

LONDON AND NEW YORK

First published 2009
by Routledge
2 Park Square, Milton Park, Abingdon, Oxon OX14 4RN

Simultaneously published in the USA and Canada
by Routledge
270 Madison Avenue, New York, NY 10016

Routledge is an imprint of the Taylor & Francis Group, an informa business

Typeset in Garamond by Keyword Group Ltd
Printed and bound in Great Britain by MPG Book Ltd, Bodmin

British Library Cataloguing in Publication Data
A catalogue record for this book is available from the British Library

Library of Congress Cataloging-in-Publication Data
Wallace, Belle.
    Teaching problem-solving and thinking skills through science:
exciting cross-curricular challenges for foundation phase, key stage one
and key stage two / Belle Wallace, Andrew Berry and Diana Cave.
        p. cm.
    Includes bibliographical references and index.
    1. Science—Study and teaching (Elementary)—Great Britain—
Activity programs. 2. Problem solving—Study and teaching
(Elementary)—Great Britain. 3. Thought and thinking—Study and
teaching (Elementary)—Great Britain. 4. Interdisciplinary approach in
education—Great Britain. I. Berry, Andrew. II. Cave, Diana. III. Title.
    LB1585.5.G7W35 2008
    372.35′044—dc22   2008019912

ISBN 10: 0-415-45035-7 (pbk)
ISBN 13: 978-0-415-45035-5 (pbk)

Contents

Acknowledgements

To the learners

The first acknowledgment must go to all the learners who, through their enjoyment in learning, inspired both the authors and the teachers. However, while all the learners in the contributing schools have contributed to this book, there have been a number who have chosen to become junior co-authors. The learners from the National School, Grantham, Lincolnshire, volunteered to review the books and websites they had used in their science project based on Space and Rockets, so that other teachers and learners could benefit from their research. The learners did this in their own time, and we intend to have a real book launch just like real writers do! In particular, Luke Michael Wren pursued his own line of investigation into robots and he has shared his research and some of his robot constructions.

Our junior co-authors are:

The National Church of England, Junior School, Lincolnshire

To my co-authors and the schools and teachers

I am personally and deeply grateful for the dedicated work of Diana Cave and Andrew Berry who have brought such depth of understanding to the TASC (Thinking Actively in a Social Context) Framework. In addition, the teachers who have contributed to this book have also been fully engaged with the TASC process and our collective debt to them is enormous. We could not have produced '*FunTASCit through Science*' without their commitment and willingness to share their planning and examples of the children's work.

Gonerby Hill Foot Church of England Primary School, Lincolnshire

Headteacher: Peter Riches

Class teachers and teaching assistants:

Reception: Amy Thorpe, Vicki Bremner, Rachel Clare, Pauline Jeffrey and Diane Smith.

Years 1 & 2: Rachel Bensley, Lisa Radford, Denise Macey, Lin Wall, Sue Sharpe and Sharon Liddiard.

Years 3 & 4: Sarah Walker, Duncan Jones, Lisa Hoyland, Sue Dowse, Tina Simmons and Diane Williams.

Years 5 & 6: Rachel Barnard, Paulette Bullock, Richard Tomlinson, Nita Johnson, Gill Noon and Karen Hannigan.

Little Gonerby Church of England Infants School, Lincolnshire

Headteacher: Elizabeth Wiggins

Class teachers and teaching assistants:

Reception: Jane Anderson, Trish Odell, Helen Jackson, Catherine Goode, Hannah Longman, Charlotte Barber and Yvonne Whitty.

Year 1: Marguerite Tibbett, Kirstie Cunningham and Jen Bayley.

Year 2: Lesley Norton, Helen Jones, Sue Coleman, Julie Close, Rosemary Betts, Yvonne Parker, Jane McDonnell and Philippa Jones.

Maun Infant and Nursery School, Nottinghamshire

Headteacher: Mary Haig

Class teachers and teaching assistants:

Foundation Phase and Years 1 and 2: Sally Pell, Rachel Fisher, Phil Somers, Rachel Otter, Anna Hadfield, Samantha Mason, Julie Westbury, Kerry Machant, Christine Taylor, Sarah Emmonds and Yvonne Fairhurst.

Ollerton Primary School, Nottinghamshire

Headteacher: Carol Gilderdale

Class teachers and teaching assistants:

Foundation Phase: Lorraine Broadley, Jen Barthorpe, Wendy Whitby, Janet Gibson and Janice Leatherland.

Years 1 and 2: Helen Myatt-Smith, Helen Morrell, Caroline Rafton, Millie Papacoullas, Jeanette Head, Helen Lonsdale and Sylvia Rose.

Year 3: Carly Asher, John Catling, Sue Reast and Karen Young.

Year 4: Sara Turner, Terence Holmes, Richard Smith, Sue Wilkinson and Sarah Belcher.

Year 5: Carl Braithwaite, Claire Hopkinson, Kate Sunderland, Kathy Jobling, Diana Snowden and Hazel Bettney.

Year 6: Louise Carpenter, Ian Bennett, Judy Blaszcyk and Carol Haynes.

The National Church of England Junior School, Lincolnshire

Headteacher: John Gibbs

Deputy headteacher: Kay Sutherland

Class teachers and teaching assistants:

Year 3: Diane Ramsay, Emily Jenkins, Laura Szymanski, Miriam Core, Carol Parker, Michelle Dixon, Lynda Kirton and Linda Mason.

Year 4: Steven Chamberlain, Diana Cave, Victoria Scatchard, Gemma Blake-Hatton, Mavis Deptford and Kathryn Franklin.

Year 5: Heather Banks, Wendy Britton, Nicola Chamberlain, David Nicholson, Karen Lambert, Julie Dowsett and Christine Farmilo.

Year 6: Elizabeth Woods, Mari Mander, Theresa Thomas, Susan Nadin, Joanne Franklin, Deanna Lawrance and Amanda Young.

Special thanks to our caretaker: Alexander Douglas.

Ropley Church of England Primary School, Hampshire

Headteacher: Clare Molyneux

Class teachers and teaching assistants:

Clare Farrell, Emma Glithro, Alison Meredith, Chris Noyce, Anne Perriam, Julie Kirkland, Kay Waterworth, Jenny Roberts, Julie Fairey, Anne Marshall, Janet Dance, Wendy Varnham, Kayleigh Brown, Julia Wills, Lesley Smith, Sue Hill, Jill Stride and Norma Day.

William Hildyard Church of England Primary School, Lincolnshire

Headteacher: Fiona Griffiths

Class teacher: Sally-Ann Lucas

I would also like to thank Harvey B. Adams for his patient and thorough editing of the text.

Introduction: Why use TASC as a framework for developing problem-solving and thinking skills?

As with all previous publications that show the TASC (Thinking Actively in a Social Context) Problem-solving Framework in action, this book has been produced with the help of many teachers and children. The TASC Framework needs to be seen in action, since it is not just a theoretical base for curriculum development, but a very practical approach to whole school development that aims to empower all children to think more effectively.

Hence, all of the examples in this book are real and practical examples of children and teachers using the TASC Framework in classrooms. All of the classrooms have children with multiple needs – a situation which is pervasive throughout our schools today. The teachers are collectively amongst the most dedicated in our profession, and I owe them all a great debt of gratitude. They have all embraced the TASC Framework and have willingly contributed to this book, being quite happy to share their planning and also carefully collecting the relevant data needed for such an illustrative book.

Importantly, all the contributing schools have excellent leaders in their head-teachers and senior management. It is quite evident when working with a school that whole school development is a team process. It is equally evident that the children are involved, have ownership of their learning, and make excellent progress, often beginning their development from way below the baseline assessment criteria. Importantly, for me, the staff and children are happy! Of course problems constantly arise, but the schools radiate a sense of 'we are working together as committed professionals for the benefit of all the children'. The 'Every Child Matters' agenda is real and can be observed daily in all the classrooms.

The TASC Framework develops whole brain activity and the more we learn about brain activity through neuro-science, the more validity is given to the TASC Framework for developing problem-solving and thinking skills. I am thrilled by this, since it confirms that 'research' into teaching and learning must start with *reflective living research* that involves teachers, parents and, most importantly, the children as equal partners. The very beginnings of the TASC Framework grew from discussions with learners about the problem-solving and thinking skills they were already using successfully; and then listening carefully to what skills they felt they needed to learn more effectively. The role of caring mentorship was essential in these discussions because often the learners were unaware of the strategies they could develop to improve their thinking. The role of the 'teacher' was one of listening, praising and making suggestions that the learners used, and then afterwards discussing the usefulness of these strategies.

Learners are more perceptive than we often realise. Of course they know when they are interested and excited about their learning and, happy, engaged children are motivated learners. Hence an important aspect of the TASC Framework is to say to learners: What do you find interesting? What questions would you like to research? How can I help you to do this? This is the very foundation of personalising and differentiating learning – the teacher is the guide and inspiration; the learner has ownership and is involved in decision-making. The skilled teacher then builds into the children's learning the vast repertoire of basic and advanced skills that are necessary.

Another vital element of the TASC message is that there are no mistakes only re-thinks! How empowering it is to know that everyone makes mistakes and that everyone is capable of correcting those mistakes! The role of the teacher is to praise every effort and then to ask those questions that allow children to re-think. In addition, the skill of the good teacher is to identify what skills the children need to make progress and to directly teach these skills, discussing with the learners why such skills are necessary.

This book includes many examples of teachers' excellent planning which shows careful and perceptive analysis of what skills the children need and what skills they are developing. Essentially the content is the servant not the master – the teacher has the overall plan in mind but the learners also have a say in what is learned and how it is learned. The learning journey is negotiable although the teacher makes the necessary professional decisions and guides appropriately.

The illustrations throughout the book are natural on-the-spot snaps of learners' reactions when they are fully involved in their learning. Nothing is posed or set up for the camera; often the learners are quite unaware that the camera is in action, although, as you will see, some learners quite enjoy the limelight!

In 2006 I carried out a survey of 350 schools that were using the TASC Framework across the curriculum. These are some of the comments made by teachers, pupils, parents and governors when they experience the effect of working within the TASC Framework.

Motivation, independence and engagement

All teachers reported that pupils' motivation and engagement with the learning tasks were increased to the point where they hardly needed to intervene in the learning activity. The TASC Framework supplied a structure which all the children were keen to engage with and the teacher's role became that of a facilitator rather than an instructor.

☐ 'I have never experienced pupils so intent on their chosen project. They were totally engaged and I did not have to keep them on task.'

☐ 'I found I was almost redundant! I had time to observe the children and saw a number of children in a new light.'

☐ 'Children who are never engaged with learning and who generally need constant supervision just got on with the task they had decided on. They were making their own decisions, I realised it was because they had ownership.'

☐ 'I have several children who are Statemented (requiring intense, usually individual, support) and several children on the Special Needs Register (requiring general learning support), but you really couldn't pick them out from the rest. They were engaged and contributing to the group.'

☐ 'The more able children took to the TASC Framework straight away and needed no extra support, but when I provided the minimum support for lower ability children, they could refer to the TASC Framework for further support. Even for these children I was just a gofer!'

☐ 'Disaffected boys are hard to motivate! But I couldn't stop them! They talked all day about their *project* – not about soccer – their usual conversation!'

Self-esteem, enjoyment and success

All teachers reflected that the children enjoyed their work, and entered fully into the celebration of their success.

☐ 'Some children who always struggle were so happy that they could just do "re-thinks"! They realised that TASC is error free because they can go backwards and forwards in the TASC Wheel and put their thinking right!'

☐ 'There is always a happy buzz when the children are working on their TASC project. They constantly ask if today is a TASC project day!'

☐ 'The celebration of their TASC work sent all children and parents home with smiling faces. We didn't rehearse their feedback to parents – the children explained the kinds of thinking they had been doing quite easily.'

☐ 'Although a lot of the discussions are class or group work based, every child created their own mini-beast. They took pride in their own creation.'

☐ 'A child who is normally the "outsider" was an accepted member of the group. I realised that he is an excellent practical problem-solver and when the group praised his work, he just beamed!'

Diminished anti-social behaviour and increased socially acceptable behaviour

All the teachers commented on the positive change in pupils' emotional and social behaviour.

☐ 'On TASC days – the Incident Book is empty! Children choose to stay in and continue at playtimes, eating their snacks and lunch while carrying on with their project.'

☐ 'My class is a very challenging class and I was sceptical that working in the TASC way would make any difference. But I was amazed at what the children already knew and how excited they were because they could choose which questions they wanted to explore. I really was surprised that they could work without arguing and shouting!'

☐ 'Some children who are the lowest in ability (language and mathematics) and who are usually very disruptive, really shone when they realised that they could solve the problem in any way they chose. The most disruptive child has shown himself to be a very able leader and he revelled in the fact that the group appointed him the leader. He worked very fairly and gently when he was monitoring the group's progress. When things went wrong, it was he who helped to sort them out.'

☐ 'We realised that the whole school attendance picked up! One parent asked what we had done to X because she got up early for school – usually she has to be nagged and dragged up!'

☐ 'A very quiet group of girls have blossomed. They are speaking up and taking the lead, whereas previously, they just got on with their work and said very little.'

General comments from the teachers

'The atmosphere in the school is very different now. We are looking at all the pupils with new eyes. The SATs (National Standard Attainment Test) only look at Literacy and Numeracy, so we drill that in the Spring term before SATs week. But we have discovered children who are very able in other ways. We are now looking at children across the full spectrum of human abilities.'

'Our very able children on the Register (language and mathematics) have exceeded all our expectations. We realised that they were just coasting. We have been amazed at what they have been able to do! But we have extended our concept of "more able" and now we celebrate every child.'

'It is so much more exciting to work in the TASC way because the children respond better. You still have to do the background planning to assemble possible resources and you still have to guide what it is possible to do in the time and space; but we share the planning with the children now, and they can understand what is possible and what is not feasible. Their questioning skills have leapt in depth and breadth!'

'Our standards in SATs have been the highest ever, and we think it is because the children are so motivated and on task. We still have to be concerned about our SATs results but we are going for the thinking first!'

General comments from the children reported by the teachers

- 'TASC Projects give us a chance to show what we can do. They are a break from school work.'

- 'TASC days are a chance to be creative and not have the teachers telling you all the time what to do.'

- 'I realised that TASC is already in my head but I didn't know it! I use the TASC wheel to guide my thinking.'

- 'TASC days "confidences us up" so we are not afraid to speak out in front of other people.'

- 'TASC gives us a full packed education! We didn't realise until afterwards that we had done research, history, ICT, art, craft, DT, drama, speaking and listening. We even did some Literacy and we enjoyed it!'

- 'TASC days are exciting because "you can open up your creative side". Teachers don't say that's wrong and it takes a lot of pressure off you.'

- 'My mind is usually disorganised and whizzing around! The TASC wheel helps me to organise my thinking better.'

Chapter 1

An explanation of TASC. How does TASC help to develop the processes of scientific thinking in learners?

Making Science a real, hands-on problem-solving learning experience

A Glimpse of Life Poised and Open in Expectancy

The eyes of a newly born child focus gradually on an awareness of a world of colours, shapes and shadows. The dawning and recognition of faces that smile and welcome, and the scent and warmth of supporting arms in the close intimacy of nurturing and caring – the first knowing of the self. The self-parted from the time of preconscious thought yet still linked to it for a brief all-knowing time. A gift to adults – these newly opened eyes – a glimpse into eternity – a glimpse of life poised and open in expectancy.

What experiences then clarify and colour in the outline of the child's new world of knowing?

What feelings quickly network through the brain's potential brilliance?

What confirming sense of being in the world confirms the premonition of joy and self as one dimension?

What will the old, worn, gnarled and cynical world of experience offer to the newly born child?

(Wallace 2006)

Designing, Gathering and Creating

All children are born with the gifts of curiosity and creativity – and the potential, usually insatiable, gift for asking questions to find out about the world in which they live. Fostering these questions and developing inquisitive and investigating minds is one of the essential roles of parent and teacher, and scientific enquiry is a wonderful route for nurturing and developing all children's potential for thoughtful discovery.

The ethos of this book is that 'Every Child Matters'. The underlying message is one of 'Inclusion with Differentiation'. The theme flowing throughout is that teachers and learners need to work interactively to construct knowledge and together, through this interaction, deep and sustained learning is promoted. When learners are truly involved in constructing knowledge for themselves, then their motivation is high and both individual and group effort is sustained. We all realise that maintaining learners' motivation and interest is the route that leads to the raising of the standards of achievement of all learners.

Intelligence is the essential capacity to solve problems – seen most dynamically through practical problem-solving activities involving creative and analytical thinking embedded within real-life topics. All children (and adults) can improve their skills of thinking and problem-solving – 'intelligence' is not fixed in any individual – we all have the capacity to improve and to grow throughout the whole of our lifetime.

Investigate with the learners

The Qualifications and Curriculum Authority (QCA) Document (QCA 2005) and *The Primary Science Education Report* (September 2005) stress the need for practical problem-solving in Science that provides differentiated levels of activities for learners. The document also suggests that when teachers become *investigators with learners*, then both the scientific processes and the end results are shared between teachers and learners. This means that the teacher does not need to be a science expert knowing all of the answers beforehand, but a co-learner engaging in open-ended problem-solving investigative science.

Personalised learning

Vitally, when children have opportunities to negotiate the topics of their investigative work, they have ownership of their learning which leads to increased motivation and attention. This is *personalising learning* – encouraging learners to find out possible answers to questions that they have raised as interesting and worth exploring. This, in turn, leads to increased confidence in questioning, a sense of self-esteem and self-worth, and the promotion of a life lived with the posing of questions and the search for possible answers to those questions.

The photographs show the model playgrounds made by children in St. Gwladys Primary School, Caerphilly, who have used the TASC process to create their own environments.

Creating Our Environment

In-depth investigations

Schools are becoming increasingly aware of the amount of repetition of scientific facts and concepts throughout the Foundation Phase and Key Stages 1 and 2. This has prompted schools to plan the science investigative work as a continuum from the Foundation Phase through to the end of Key Stage 2 – not only cutting out unnecessary repetition, but importantly, creating time and space for sustained in-depth science investigations. Of course, this is not to suggest that children do not have to learn basic subject skills, research and recording skills and ICT skills – these skills are the basic skills that underpin all open-ended investigations and explorations at Primary level, and they equip learners with the necessary interest and skills to engage in rigorous investigations and explorations at Key Stages 3, 4 and 5. Ultimately we want learners who persevere, are independent and who are driven by curiosity about the world in which they live.

Differentiated learning

It is ideal and best practice that enables differentiated learning to become a reality in the classroom. Since the TASC Framework provides a structure for learners to work independently or in small groups, then learners can take the topic, investigation or research project into as much the depth and breadth as they choose. The TASC Framework replicates, albeit very simply, how an expert thinker thinks and since the world is a 'mixed ability' world, individual learners will need different levels of support. Some learners will use the TASC Framework to fly independently and will require minimum teacher support. Other learners will need quite strong scaffolding and support, but working through the stages of the TASC Wheel gives them the overall structure for the processes of their thinking and problem-solving.

Relevant to life

The key to arousing and sustaining interest in science lies in making science more relevant to children's lives, investigating everyday scientific concepts. The obvious importance of scientific understanding of the world around us is constantly increasing as we are bombarded with science and technology as an integral part of our everyday lives. This does not mean buying extensive and costly scientific equipment, but means using a basic range of measuring tools and simple science equipment, together with junk materials that children can collect themselves. Additionally, scientific investigations can be located in stories, role-play, drama, history, geography, maths, literacy, and cross-curricular projects. The National Primary Strategy in England states that 'There is no requirement for subjects to be taught discretely – they can be grouped, or taught in projects' (*DfES May, 2003*).

The children at Cwmaber Junior School, Caerphilly, have used the TASC Framework to create their own litter bins to keep their school neat and tidy.

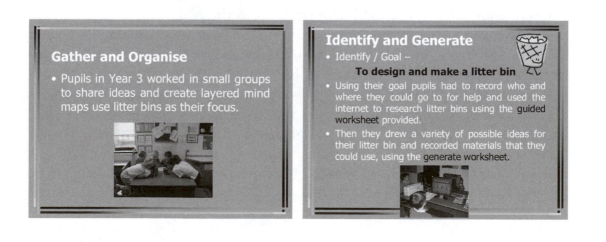

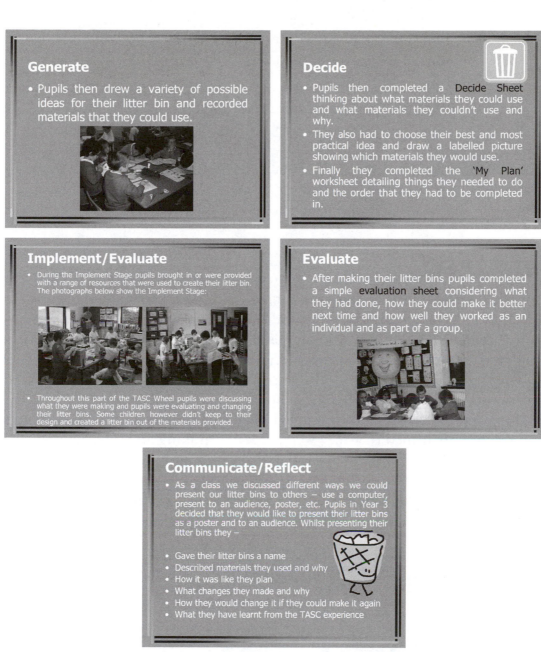

The aims of this text are to:

☐ provide suggestions for practical classroom projects that involve children in investigating everyday scientific concepts;

☐ guide teachers and learners through the scientific processes of the investigations;

☐ suggest cross-curricular projects drawing out the possibilities for scientific explorations;

☐ suggest cross-curricular projects linked in a topic web to the main science topic;

☐ suggest avenues of exploration that reach out for greater depth and breadth;

□   provide practical guidelines for teacher assessment and for pupil self-assessment, tracking and target setting;

□   give examples of a wide range of recording techniques that require maximum thinking and minimum recording;

□   indicate possibilities for linking science investigations with ICT;

□   develop scientific literacy and a range of scientific language for thinking and problem-solving.

Why *TASC*?

Together with Harvey Adams, throughout the 1980s, I searched the world for a well-founded and sustainable rationale that could underpin a whole curriculum that developed problem-solving and thinking skills. Visiting countries that were beginning to dabble in 'thinking skills'; working with researchers delving into the concept of 'intelligence'; working alongside 'expert thinkers' and asking them to externalise their thought processes; and most importantly, trialling and constantly revising strategies and thinking tools until both learners and teachers identified that they were, indeed, thinking and solving problems efficiently and successfully.[1] Since then, the emerging field of neuro-science has increasingly confirmed that when the brain is fully and actively engaged in learning, then pupils are both motivated and persevering when they have relevant problems to solve.

TASC means 'Thinking Actively in a Social Context'

Thinking

All children can *think,* but thinking can be enhanced and developed through appropriate practice, like a gymnast trains and perfects complex movements so that they become automatic and controlled but also highly flexible and creative.

Actively

Every child needs to be an *active* thinker! We can't '*do* thinking to a child'!

We need to engage children in activities that involve them in their own thinking and problem-solving, letting them see that these thinking activities are qualitatively different from rote learning and practice, important though these activities are.

Social

Children are so good at teaching each other! We are *social* beings and when we are communicating we are crystallising ideas. Children can and do teach each other, often explaining and making meaning amongst themselves in a far more comprehensible way than when teacher explains.

Context

When learning is in the *context* of real life experience, then learners can identify with the topic and develop ownership, and also relate to the learning in a personal way because it has relevance.

Working through science investigations, linking learning to life and engaging children in real problem-solving, not only is the TASC way of working, but also the key to raising achievement and firing motivation.

Copyright © Belle Wallace 2000

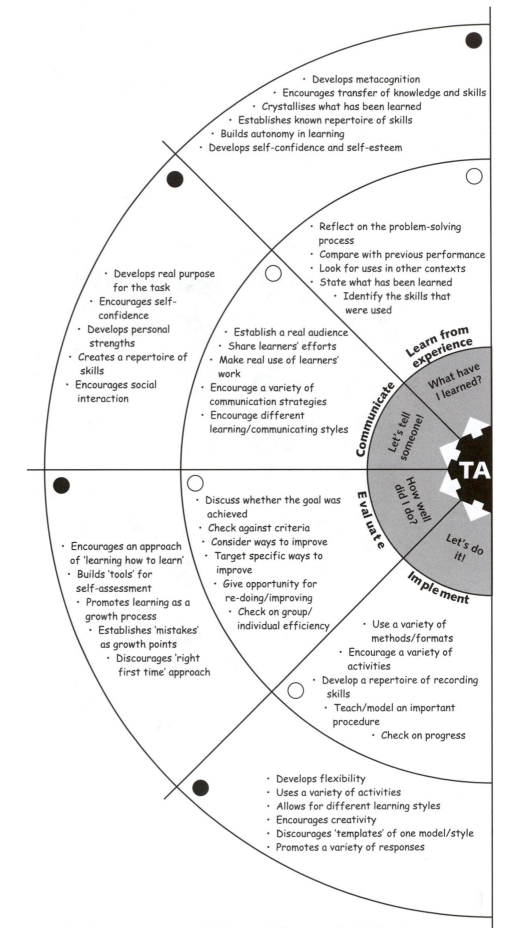

Develops metacognition
• Encourages transfer of knowledge and skills
• Crystallises what has been learned
• Establishes known repertoire of skills
• Builds autonomy in learning
• Develops self-confidence and self-esteem

• Develops real purpose
  for the task
• Encourages self-
  confidence
• Develops personal
  strengths
• Creates a repertoire of
  skills
• Encourages social
  interaction

• Reflect on the problem-solving
  process
• Compare with previous performance
• Look for uses in other contexts
• State what has been learned
• Identify the skills that
  were used

• Establish a real audience
• Share learners' efforts
• Make real use of learners'
  work
• Encourage a variety of
  communication strategies
• Encourage different
  learning/communicating styles

Learn from experience
What have I learned?

Communicate
Let's tell someone!

TA

Evaluate
How well did I do?

Let's do it!

Implement

• Encourages an approach
  of 'learning how to learn'
• Builds 'tools' for
  self-assessment
• Promotes learning as a
  growth process
• Establishes 'mistakes'
  as growth points
• Discourages 'right
  first time' approach

• Discuss whether the goal was
  achieved
• Check against criteria
• Consider ways to improve
• Target specific ways to
  improve
• Give opportunity for
  re-doing/improving
• Check on group/
  individual efficiency

• Use a variety of
  methods/formats
• Encourage a variety of
  activities
• Develop a repertoire of recording
  skills
• Teach/model an important
  procedure
• Check on progress

• Develops flexibility
• Uses a variety of activities
• Allows for different learning styles
• Encourages creativity
• Discourages 'templates' of one model/style
• Promotes a variety of responses

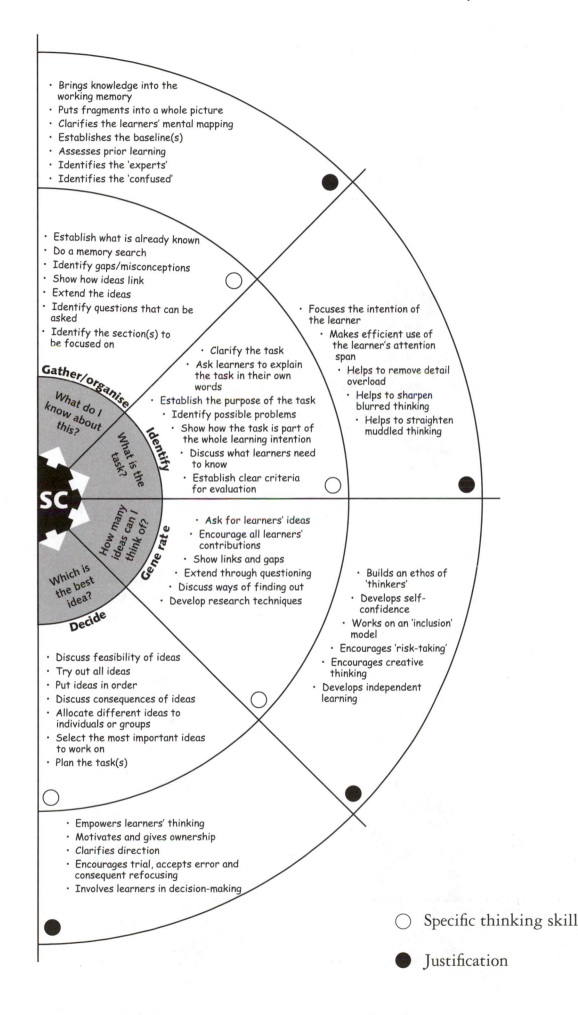

- Brings knowledge into the working memory
- Puts fragments into a whole picture
- Clarifies the learners' mental mapping
- Establishes the baseline(s)
- Assesses prior learning
- Identifies the 'experts'
- Identifies the 'confused'

- Establish what is already known
- Do a memory search
- Identify gaps/misconceptions
- Show how ideas link
- Extend the ideas
- Identify questions that can be asked
- Identify the section(s) to be focused on

- Focuses the intention of the learner
- Makes efficient use of the learner's attention span
- Helps to remove detail overload
- Helps to sharpen blurred thinking
- Helps to straighten muddled thinking

Gather/organise

What do I know about this?

Identify

What is the task?

SC

How many ideas can I think of?

Generate

Which is the best idea?

Decide

- Clarify the task
- Ask learners to explain the task in their own words
- Establish the purpose of the task
- Identify possible problems
- Show how the task is part of the whole learning intention
- Discuss what learners need to know
- Establish clear criteria for evaluation

- Ask for learners' ideas
- Encourage all learners' contributions
- Show links and gaps
- Extend through questioning
- Discuss ways of finding out
- Develop research techniques

- Builds an ethos of 'thinkers'
- Develops self-confidence
- Works on an 'inclusion' model
- Encourages 'risk-taking'
- Encourages creative thinking
- Develops independent learning

- Discuss feasibility of ideas
- Try out all ideas
- Put ideas in order
- Discuss consequences of ideas
- Allocate different ideas to individuals or groups
- Select the most important ideas to work on
- Plan the task(s)

- Empowers learners' thinking
- Motivates and gives ownership
- Clarifies direction
- Encourages trial, accepts error and consequent refocusing
- Involves learners in decision-making

○ Specific thinking skill

● Justification

Using and recording the TASC process

How to use TASC

All the stages of the TASC Problem-solving Framework can be conducted with the whole class, or with small groups. More able learners quickly learn to use the TASC Framework easily and independently, while other learners use the TASC Framework as strong scaffolding for the stages of their learning. Classroom assistants are a great help in using the TASC Framework when they are supporting learners with special needs: the learners are encouraged to do the thinking orally, while the adult does the necessary recording.

If the work is mainly oral, as it is with young learners, then either the exact words of the children can be quickly jotted down on a flip chart or whiteboard and saved, or a short memo of their ideas can be made afterwards – this is the *evidence* available, for *anyone* to read, of the learning that is taking place. When children are able to write, then the recording of the thinking in each stage needs to be minimal. The guide is: 'Maximum thinking; Minimum recording'. Obviously, children can also record through drawing, tape-recording, on white-boards, or on TASC project boards. Where appropriate, records of the TASC process can be photographed. Mindmaps, plans, 're-thinks' and finished work can also be photocopied for every child so that they have a copy of the stages of their collective thinking to paste into their books as *evidence* that they have been actively engaged in the process of problem-solving.

It is important to record in some way *all* stages of the TASC process and indicate that these stages are the 'thinking stages': then the finished result is marked 'final product'. It is a good idea to mark all the thinking with a green sticker and the finished product with a red sticker. This highlights and celebrates the thinking and children soon realise that the thinking is the most important part of learning.

Thinking

The TASC Framework itself provides the 'control' of the lesson(s). However, when children are working within the TASC Framework, teachers universally report that learners are 'on task' with increased attention and concentration. Many 'behaviour problems' disappear, as learners become more engaged in taking more responsibility for their thinking and decision-making. Moreover, in any TASC based activity, learning objectives can be easily 'slotted in', selected appropriately from across the curriculum.

Creating and using the TASC Wheel

Linking TASC with brain activity

The processes encapsulated within the TASC Framework correspond with the latest theories of neuro-science that confirm how children best learn and, consequently, how teachers best teach.

Stages of the TASC Framework

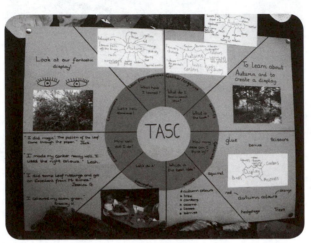

Thinking about thinking

Gather and Organise

Gather and organise: What do I know already?

This stage encourages learners to pull the fragments of their learning into the working memory. There are no mistakes in this activity: all children are successful, although some of the remembering may be fragmented. The important element in this stage is to draw the connecting lines between ideas. Mindmaps are vitally important since they replicate, through both simple and complex formats, how the brain actually functions; and the more often children use mindmaps, flowcharts and diagrams of all sorts, the better they can make the links in their learning. This activity also helps memory and recall since the very making of a mindmap activates, reinforces and links the neurons, strengthening the connections in the brain. Post-it notes are very useful for first gathering and then organising and grouping ideas because they can be re-arranged – but again the links must be shown to emphasise how the ideas are connected.

Ideas

With young learners, this stage can be developed and practised through gathering and organising a collection of tangible objects around a broad theme, for example, model vehicles, small toys, collections of various bottle tops or large buttons. The items are stored in a big box ready for sorting into groups in as many ways as is possible. In these activities, we need to sort out the items on the floor and then use coloured ribbons to represent the connecting lines – a tangible, hands-on, changeable, visible mindmap. Or, as many early years practitioners can demonstrate – large hoops arranged in a Venn Diagram showing similarities and differences is an ideal strategy for gathering and then organising in a variety of ways. The concepts of weight, volume, shape, size, colour, usefulness, interest, old and new, can all be taught and easily learned through practical gathering and organising.

Sorting

If we know that learners have little prior experience to 'gather' from, then it is important to flood the experiential learning *before* doing a 'gather and organise'. For example, if children are going to be doing an investigation of 'Habitats', it is important to visit a nature park, a forest, a seaside, or a riverbank, etc. Then children have a rich store of experiences from which to gather and organise what they already know. It is helpful to let the children take a series of digital photographs of the exploration or visit. These photographs can be easily and quickly be transferred on to a whiteboard, and they enable immediate recall and can be used for a range of different activities. An emphasis on first hand experience is essential for learners of all ages as they build a bank of rich learning activities that prompt recall and establish reference points. The 'gather and organise stage' of the TASC helps to develop confidence in 'playing with ideas' and also in the development of the skill of 'reflecting back' at a later stage of the TASC cycle.

In this early stage of the TASC cycle, it is also important to look for cross-curricular links through stories, drama, dance, music, numeracy, literacy, art, craft and design, etc.

Identify

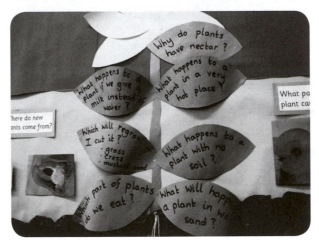

Identify

Identify: What am I going to do?

The brain needs to focus on the direction and purpose of the learning. Often, it is necessary to identify *for* the children the broad topic they are going to explore and learn about; and then to discuss with them, the essential specific skills they will need to learn in order to pursue their investigation. But as often as possible, children need to identify the area of their exploration for themselves which personalises their learning and gives them a sense of ownership.

Important questions are:

☐   What would you like to know about this topic?

☐   What questions could we ask?

☐   What would you like to find out?

☐   How could you find out?

For example, after the rich experiential learning mentioned prior to the investigation of 'Habitats', children could be asked to identify particular questions that they would like to explore further.

Helping children to identify their own avenues of interest and exploration is a powerful motivator for learning: it focuses the direction of exploration and generates the emotional involvement needed for attention and concentration. It is also the critical point for differentiation: some children can tackle simpler tasks, while others work in greater depth and breadth.

Alongside the identification of the task, pupils need to begin to discuss questions such as: How will I know that my work is good or excellent? What should it look like when I have finished? This kind of questioning links the purpose of the task with the end goal. The brain understands where the learning is leading – the direction, both logical and creative, of the learning journey.

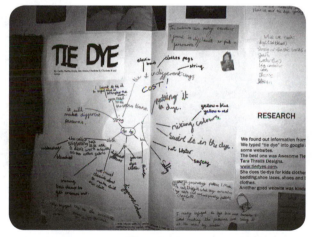

Generate

Generate: How many ways can I do it?

This is the highly creative stage of generating possibilities and the brain is very actively making numerous cross-connecting links. Children enjoy 'generating' because there are no 'wrong ideas' and they become very enthusiastic and highly motivated. Again, this stage of thinking engenders a sense of ownership and personalisation. The children are suggesting possible avenues for the development of their activities and making their own decisions, rather than the teacher directing the activity. There are a number of key questions such as:

☐   What do I need to know in order to do this?

☐   Where can I find out?

☐   Who can I ask?

☐   How many ways can I do this?

☐   How shall I present/communicate my work?

If children are reticent to suggest possibilities, or lack the confidence, then the role of the teacher is to enter into the excitement of generating ideas, modelling a range of possible avenues for exploration. By doing this, the teacher can 'manoeuvre' the discussion and very subtly direct the range of activities to be developed.

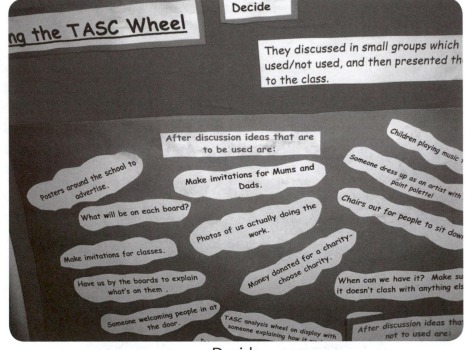

Decide

Decide: Which are the best ideas?

After a very creative exploration of possibilities, the brain needs to think more logically and decide which ideas are feasible and possible. This stage still allows for creative decision-making, but the decision is more focused towards the end goal. Important questions include:

☐   Which is the best way to do this?

☐   Will it be a fair test? How and why?

☐   Is there only one variable? What is it?

☐   How am I going to measure my results?

☐   What is the plan of action?

☐   What materials do I need?

☐   How much time have I got?

Plan

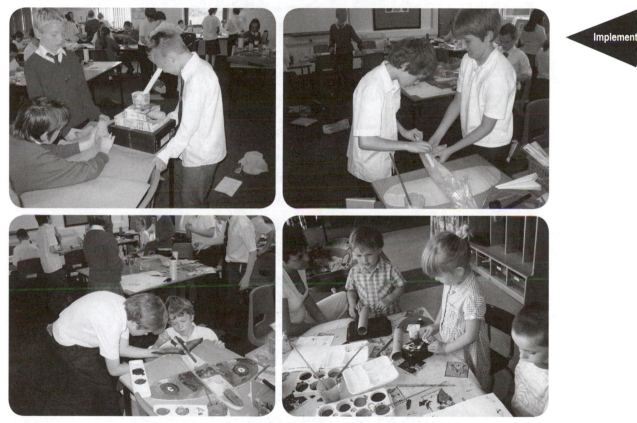

Implement

Implement: Let's do it!

This is the time to think about ways of putting the decision to action! Learners should already have some ideas of how they want to pursue their enquiry and also how they want to present or communicate their work from discussions at the generate stage. Vitally, all children should have opportunities, over half a term or a term, to present their work using their strong abilities. By working across the full range of human abilities: social, emotional, spiritual, mechanical/technical, scientific, auditory/musical, visual/spatial, movement, and linguistic (oral and written), mathematical; all children have a chance to shine and celebrate what they can do well.

The brain is capable of functioning across and within *all* the human abilities and we combine several abilities in everything we do, but we also have different profiles of strengths that are partly genetically endowed and partly environmentally fostered.

Often, learners who need support in Literacy and Numeracy shine brightly when engaged in using their other abilities and it is essential that they have opportunities to show their strengths if their interest and motivation is to be maintained.

Evaluate

Evaluate

Record using ICT

Evaluate: How well did I do?

Of course teacher observation, assessment and evaluation are necessary; but if we are to develop pupil ownership, decision-making and personalised learning, then pupils need to learn how to evaluate both their own and also each others' work. Being able to evaluate one's effort is a major key to autonomy in learning. The brain needs to acknowledge success, which is a powerful factor in building self-confidence, whilst simultaneously accommodating the need for improvement and further learning. This process not only demands critical thinking, but also deep emotional strength and self-esteem. In a classroom that celebrates success across all human abilities, it is easier for learners to acknowledge that they need to improve and strengthen certain abilities.

Learners praising each other's efforts, while offering an idea for improvement, begins the process of self-evaluation. But it is also necessary that learners know what 'competence' and 'excellence' look like and providing learners with concrete examples that they can discuss is an essential route for developing this evaluative capacity across all subjects within the curriculum and outside it.

Communicate

Communicate: Let's share what we have learned!

In sharing ideas, learners are crystallising what they know and what they have learned. In explaining to other children, learners are ordering and manipulating their ideas so that others can understand. In addition, it is wonderful fun to share using a variety of methods and skills, and importantly, children are learning new ideas from each other.

We are social beings and reaching out to interact with others develops our social, emotional and spiritual strengths as well as our cognitive abilities. When we communicate, we have the opportunity to use the whole brain – both creatively and logically across all dimensions of human abilities. Importantly, children are 'doing something exciting' with their learning rather than just always 'writing it down'.

Moreover, when learners communicate across the full range of human abilities, their skills of literacy also improve. Since what they are communicating is the product of *their own thinking*, they can more easily talk about it and as a result, more easily write about it.

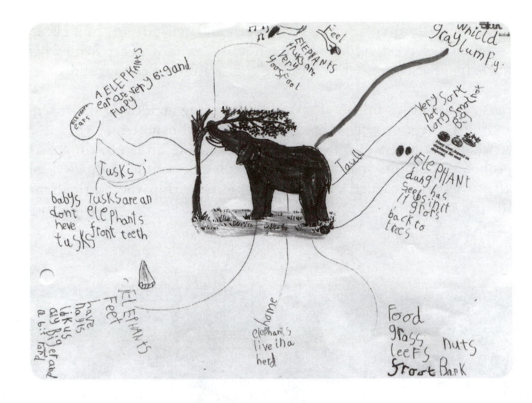

Learn from experience: What have we learned?

This is the metacognitive stage – the thinking about thinking, feeling and learning. The brain has the wonderful capacity for 'looking down on itself', in order to reflect on its own functioning. All learners need to realise that they are making progress: it is not only the children who receive learning support who need to realise this; but also the more able learners need to realise that they are extending their learning and not just marking time.

At the end of a topic or piece of work, important discussion should take place centring round questions such as:

☐   What do I know now that I didn't know before?

☐   What new skills have I learned?

☐   How else can I use these skills?

☐   How can I improve my way of working?

☐   How can I improve how I work with others?

It is essential to return to the original mindmap of the 'gather and organise' stage and add in any new ideas or knowledge. This extends the original brain map of where the learner started and helps with training memory and with later recall of what has been learned.

When we can articulate what we have learned, then we can understand the learning that has taken place.

Linking the TASC way of working directly with the specific skills of science

The specific skills needed for scientific enquiry dovetail neatly into the TASC Framework. For example:

Fair testing fits easily into the TASC stages of gather and organise, identify, generate, decide, evaluate, communicate, with questions such as:

☐ What do I know already?

☐ What have I already observed?

☐ Which is the best way to do this?

☐ Is there only one variable?

☐ Do I have a control?

☐ How am I going to record and compare my results?

☐ What further questions can I ask?

☐ How will I be able to justify my findings?

☐ Is my result always going to be the same?

Pattern-seeking and surveying are also essential TASC Tools and apply to all subjects across the curriculum, when we ask questions such as:

☐ Is this true in every example?

☐ Which are the 'odd ones out'? Why?

☐ What is the general rule?

Classifying and identifying are the most fundamental and basic thinking skills that allow us to compare and contrast and make sense of any information. This kind of thinking is particularly needed for the Gather and Organise, Evaluate and Learn from Experience Stages of the TASC Process. Questions such as the following are also cross-curricular:

☐ How can I group these ideas?

☐ Which characteristics are the same?

☐ Which characteristics are different?

☐ What is usual? Unusual?

☐ Which characteristics remain constant? Change?

Investigations over time allow for extended work in depth and breadth. This extended period of time for study fits the TASC Framework particularly well

Basic and Advanced Thinking Skills and Strategies (Tools)

TASC	Gather and Organise	Identify	Generate	Decide
Key Questions	What do I already know about this? Make links and group ideas together. Maybe organise information as a mind map.	What are we trying to do? What are our success criteria? How will we know if we have done a good job? What do we need to do this?	How many ways can we do this? Who can we ask to help us? Where can we find out? Let's all think about this.	Which is the best way? What should we do first? Why should we do it this way? What will happen if we do this?
Advanced Thinking Skills	Searching memory; recalling from past experiences; recalling from recent stimuli; Hitch-hiking onto others' ideas; Organising links.	Clarifying goals; considering success criteria; consulting others.	Creating a 'think-tank'; considering end product and research possibilities; consulting others.	Looking at both sides of an idea; exploring the consequences; considering all factors; prioritising; hypothesising; predicting; consulting others.
Useful Strategies (Tools)	Ordering pictures; branch diagrams; mind mapping; bubble maps; deliberate mistakes; KWHL grids; follow-me cards; true or false cards; concept cartoons.	Think-Pair-Share; flowcharts; forcefield analysis; 'What? When? Where? Why? How?'	Thought showers; hitch-hiking; concept maps; creative connections; graphical metaphors; forced metaphors.	Think-Pair-Share; ranking charts; flowcharts; practical, not practical; SWOT Analysis.
Higher Order Thinking Skills	Organising; linking knowledge, senses and feelings.	Questioning; re-phrasing suggestions; initiating ideas.	Generating ideas; questioning; comparing and contrasting.	Reasoning; questioning; clarifying; disagreeing; justifying; revising ideas; decision-making; planning.
Repertoire of Basic Thinking Skills	*These basic thinking skills need to be taught, practised and developed and form the basic* verbs, adverbs, nouns, adjectives in different contexts across the curriculum. communication and recording skills. Rich repertoire of varied sensory experiential			

The extended TASC process showing how sections of the TASC Problem-solving Processes blend into a coherent whole

Implement	Evaluate	Communicate	Learn from Experience
Is our plan working? Should we change anything? What do we do next?	Are we pleased with this? Have we done it well? Have we achieved our success criteria? How could we do it better?	Who can we tell about this? How can we show other people? How can we explain? How can we make it interesting?	What have we learned to do? How else can we use this? How do we feel now? What are we proud of?
Interpreting; applying; creating; designing; investigating; composing; consulting others.	Observing, interacting and responding to others; appraising process and product; consulting others.	Presenting; demonstrating; explaining; clarifying; justifying; consulting others.	Reflecting; making connections; transferring across the curriculum; crystallising; consolidating; extending.
Think-Pair-Share; planning grids; flowcharts; sketches.	Think-Pair-Share; extend Mindmaps; 3 Stars and a wish; next steps.	Recording across the multiple abilities: displays, performances, visuals, structures, role-plays, recordings, video clips, games.	Think-Pair-Share; extend Mindmaps; 3 Stars and a wish; consequences.
Organising; reviewing; monitoring; questioning; re-thinking Developing ideas; adapting.	Evaluating; questioning; assessing; judging.	Summarising; sharing; expressing ideas and opinions.	Reflecting; generalising; summarising.

building blocks for thinking and problem-solving. Appropriate, fluent use of prepositions, conjunctions, Appropriate use of basic concepts in number, measures, shape, space. Appropriate use of basic learning

© *Belle Wallace (2008) Teachers Problem-Solving and Thinking Skills through Science.*

since it encourages individual and small group work that is rigorously planned and recorded. Extended work requires perseverance and sound planning – essential to the Decide and Implement TASC Stages. The following questions are important:

☐   How shall I measure and record change?

☐   How often do I need to do this?

Design, test and adapt This activity is a classical TASC activity, involving the whole TASC Process, perhaps more fully than any other activity across the curriculum. It is an ideal activity for introducing learners to the whole TASC Problem-solving process in a practical, hands-on way.

Exploration of any idea again involves the whole TASC Process, focusing particularly on the skills of questioning, researching, recording and culminating in the TASC Stages of Communicate and Learn from Experience.

However, having shown the key links between the TASC process and specific scientific skills, in the lesson examples that follow in the next chapters, although the science topic will lead and centralise the planning, the pupils' activities will also show related cross-curricular links.

It is not possible to list all the components that comprise the TASC Problem-solving processes but the comprehensive diagram (on p. 30 and 31) gives examples of how the elements within the TASC Framework are blended into a coherent and whole set of educational experiences. Many teachers are over-whelmed by the constant range of new initiatives from the government and other outside agencies and say that they have difficulty fitting the pieces of the jigsaw together. Hence the purpose of the diagram is to show how these 'pieces of the jigsaw' fit together within the TASC Framework.

Basic and advanced thinking skills

The full range of the TASC Basic Thinking Skills are developed during early years' educational experiences: many of these are 'discovered', verbalised, and clarified through experiential learning; whilst others need to be *directly taught and practised*. Learners cannot learn without having mastered a wide range of Basic Thinking Skills so that they have a repertoire of 'tools' for action and problem-solving. For example, in science, learners need to learn how to measure and weigh accurately, how to manipulate simple language and number concepts and to learn scientific routines and styles of recording.

These Basic Thinking Skills evolve into Advanced Thinking Skills as learners gain mastery and confidence: the language, number and scientific skills become deeper and more complex.

Strategies (tools) for effective learning

There is a vast range of research and recording skills that make thinking easier – these are the tools that clarify the thought processes and enable children to externalise and *show* their thinking. These range from simple strategies such as verbal and visual flowcharts to more complex strategies such as the Six Thinking Hats (de Bono) which encourages learners to role-play and Philosophy for Children (Lipman) which is an excellent strategy for developing questioning and reflection.

Higher order thinking

Teachers often ask how Bloom's Taxonomy of Higher Order Thinking fits into the TASC Framework, so I have included a breakdown of the Higher Order Thinking Skills within the TASC Problem-solving Framework. I maintain, however, that *all* children can engage in *higher order thinking* if the context is relevant. Moreover, I argue that it is not a hierarchy of thinking skills but a compendium of skills that we use interactively as the context and need arises. For example, early years' children are quite capable of using higher order thinking when they analyse the sequence of events in the fairy story of Cinderella; create a different ending; and discuss the fairness of Cinderella's role as the family skivvy!

In Chapter 2, we show how planning a science topic across the curriculum incorporates the full range of multiple abilities and also the full range of Basic and Advanced Thinking Skills, together with appropriate strategies for researching and recording.

Notes

1. The theory underpinning TASC has been fully written up elsewhere. See the TASC publications and TASC classroom products listed in Appendix 1.

References

The Primary Science Education Report (September 2005)

QCA (2005) Science. 2004/5 *Annual report on curriculum and assessment. QCA/05/2177*. Available: www.qca.org.uk/libraryAssests/media/science_2004_5_annual_report_on_curriculum_and_assessment(1).pdf

Wallace B. (2006) Diversity in Gifted Education: International Perspectives on Global Issues. Oxford: Routledge.

Chapter 2

Detailed planning guidelines for a cross curricular TASC week based on Space and Rockets

Using a scientific theme to inspire and motivate all learners

We are sentient, dynamic beings capable of change; but we can be trapped not only in the learned sense of what we are not, but also in a powerful negative mirror image of ourselves that we perceive emanating from others. Yet, we can be released through enabling interactions with those special mentors who offer constant and strong scaffolding that we are, indeed, of great worth and significance as individuals with potential.

Paulo Freire crystallized for me what was, until then, only half formulated in my mind, and clarified what I was trying to achieve as a young teacher, broadly:

☐ The development of learners' ownership of their learning through the negotiation of relevant problems to be solved in relation to real life understanding;

☐ The development of dialogue and interaction in the learning/teaching dynamic with reciprocity and equality of teachers and learners as jointly negotiating and constructing meaning;

☐ The development of learners' self-confidence and independence in decision-making and actions leading to their self-actualisation;

☐ The mutual respect derived from active listening and talking.

Sadly, much of what is called 'education' falls neatly and very aptly within the framework of the Freire's 'banking' concept, it is a series of acts of:

'depositing, in which the students are the depositories and the teacher is the depositor. Instead of communicating, the teacher issues communiqués and makes deposits which the students patiently receive, memorise and repeat' (Freire, P. 1998)

Wallace (in press)

The National CE Junior School Lincolnshire

The National is a four-form entry Church of England (CE) junior school of almost 500 pupils drawn from a wide range of socio-economic backgrounds in a Lincolnshire market town. The aim of the school is to provide a happy, secure and stimulating learning environment where children are valued as individuals and are encouraged to fully develop their potential across the full range of human abilities: mathematic, linguistic, scientific, visual/spatial, auditory/musical, physical, mechanical/technical, emotional, social and spiritual within a Christian ethos. The school's aim is to discover and celebrate the gift(s) in every child, and celebrate practical ability as well as academic ability. For too long, practical ability has been sidelined or given low status, whereas, in most of us it is our strongest ability. The TASC Framework is always introduced to incoming pupils through practical, fun based, hands-on activities, so that the pressure of 'getting it right' is diminished, and the pupils can concentrate on 'thinking about thinking'. Then, as often as possible, full TASC explorations are repeated, whilst referring to stages of the TASC Wheel as appropriate throughout the curriculum.

We have the same multiple challenges as most other schools: under-developed home language, fragmented family situations, lack of experiential learning, and frequently, many pupils with poor self-esteem and self-confidence. Although we have very good relations with our feeder schools and the pupils make good progress from their baseline assessment, various kinds of under-development can only be redressed with time. Children do not suddenly change their behaviour; and since the pre-school, formative years are so influential, the brain often needs to 'unlearn' certain kinds of responses and to 're-learn' more effective behaviours.

As well as supporting pupils with special learning needs, we also have the challenge of extending some highly able pupils – we have the full range of potential from those children who need strong support to those children who are capable of flying high.

The TASC Problem-solving Framework provides scaffolding and support for those children who need it, often the teaching assistant acting as mentor and scribe; but TASC also provides a framework that allows the most able learners to work independently and to pursue an individual enquiry of special interest.

Note: The reviews of books and websites in the following chapter were written voluntarily by pupils who were thrilled to share their learning with other children, and excited at the idea of being 'authors'.

Pupils transfer from two feeder infant schools and on completing KS2, transfer to various local secondary schools, including selective grammar schools. The ethnic composition is 90 per cent White-British. Twenty per cent of pupils are identified on the SEN register, of which two per cent have a Statement of needs. Twenty-five per cent of pupils appear on the G&T register across the spectrum of the multiple abilities listed above, although we constantly monitor individual development.

The children are grouped into 16 mixed ability classes, 4 per year, within an old, largely Victorian building. Accommodation is very limited, resulting in a fairly inflexible subject-driven timetable. Any flexibility, therefore, has to be carefully orchestrated and timetabled and agreed upon by the whole staff, for example, use of the school hall, the music room and the computer suite are timetabled. Ability setting occurs in Literacy and Mathematics, with Teaching Assistants supporting pupils in lower sets and those with Statements.

The SIP curriculum and pupil learning priorities are diverse, as stated above, and include raising pupils' achievement through 'Thinking for Learning' strategies using TASC as a base. The head and deputy actively value, encourage and support the development of TASC in our school. All classes display the TASC Wheel prominently and a specially targeted TASC Week is a regular feature of our school year. It takes place annually in the autumn term and for the last few years, has occurred just before the October half-term break. Having enjoyed previous TASC weeks on the themes of 'Community', 'Travel' and 'Aztecs', possible themes for the next TASC Week are always discussed and the broad theme of 'Space' was subsequently chosen by staff for the Autumn term 2007.

Naturally, TASC Week planning is undertaken using the TASC Wheel. During the initial staff meeting at the end of summer term, we conducted a preliminary gathering and organising activity, drawing on the previous TASC Weeks, for example, What do we already know from our previous experience of TASC Weeks? What works well? What do we need to re-think? What do we already know about the needs of the pupils? What areas of the curriculum can be covered in a full TASC Week?

From this general discussion, we identified the theme of 'Space' as rich enough to enable us to create exciting activities that would spread across the full range of multiple abilities. Focus groups were established to consider the resources we had already and the resources we might possibly need. The focus groups, led by the teacher 'specialist', generated ideas for possible activities, then decisions were made with regard to activities that were possible in the time available. This broad pre-planning is necessary so as to locate good websites, plan ahead any visits and order special resources. However, the pupils are also encouraged to pursue any line of individual research or self chosen group activity if this is at all possible.

Outreach visits from The National Space Centre were booked and, early in the autumn term, planning began in earnest. Each member of staff was involved in two focus groups which met during designated staff meetings. Subject leaders led the groups which consisted of staff from each year group. Using the TASC Framework, staff enthusiastically drafted lesson plans which were kept as open-ended as possible to enable the children and the staff to interpret the final outcomes creatively. Participation in vertical groups not only increased overall levels of engagement and ownership, but also became a forum for discussing differentiation with subject leaders and increased the capacity to locate and/or create exciting and stimulating resources.

Acting as TASC Week coordinator, I held an interim meeting with the subject leaders, to gain an overall impression of the week, to ensure that the activities were interesting, manageable and varied, that duplication was avoided, and to identify timetable and resource requirements and any additional funding costs. This meeting was also an opportunity for critical reading of plans by teachers who had not been directly involved in their production. As a result, statements within the draft plans were amended and clarified before further meetings between myself as TASC Week coordinator and individual subject leaders. At these meetings, each specific lesson plan was refined and prepared for inclusion in the TASC Week planning booklet. This booklet was then shared with staff during a full staff meeting in which subject leaders responded to any queries. Final discussions took place in year group teams before more detailed differentiation, appropriate to each particular class, was inserted by the class teacher. Discussions continued throughout TASC Week itself, with additional tips and resources emerging at every conceivable opportunity.

The Outreach sessions led by the National Space Centre provided an effective introduction to the theme and were enjoyed by the children. However, because of pupil numbers, there was less opportunity for all children to actively participate in the sessions than had been expected. As a result, a last minute revision of the proposed science activity proved necessary to equip the children with the experiential learning to be able to tackle the Mechanical/ Technical activity scheduled for later in the week. Furthermore, one year group had to concentrate all the TASC activities into four days as they had booked a visiting speaker to spend a whole day with each class during the week. Organising timetabling and resource delivery in a rabbit warren of a school of 16 classes with one hall is an interesting experience. Despite building in a half-day of catch-up time at the end of the week for most year groups, there is little scope for delay when passing resources to the next class. The knowledge that some teachers accommodate eleventh-hour adjustments or hold-ups more easily than others can hang like the sword of Damocles over any coordinator!

As the vast majority of TASC Week planning is completed a few weeks before-hand, there is relatively little preparation or marking to complete during the week itself. Extensive opportunities for hands-on participation, communication, evaluation, assessment and reflection abound. The children, and teachers with any social constructivist tendencies, are in their element. However, I have become increasingly aware that where the activities nudge individuals out of their comfort zone, TASC Week can seem long and demanding. If power within the classroom normally resides entirely with the teacher, then the hardest thing for those teachers is to allow the pupils to direct their own learning as far as is possible. Moreover, the children are not used to thinking independently, making decisions and taking the initiative, and they initially need support until they gain confidence. Whereas, those teachers who like to create learning with the children, say that they find TASC week exhilarating and exciting.

Communication levels are at their highest in TASC Week. The children emerge from classrooms bursting to share news of their latest activity with equally excited friends from other classes eager to describe what they have just done. Numerous informal discussions take place between staff, exchanging anecdotes, ideas and experiences and asking for any help that is needed. On-going lesson evaluations and reflections are recorded and are discussed in a lively staff meeting following the week. Importantly, TASC Week has also become Governors' Week at our school, where steady streams of visitors arrive to share this whole-school celebration of active learning. Many comment wistfully, 'I wish that school had been like this when I was a child'. Parents frequently report that their children 'love TASC week' and 'can't wait to get to school' and how they 'hear more about the things their children do in school in TASC Week than in the rest of the year'. Pupils also appreciate the adventure of exploring open ended activities and taking responsibility for their learning. One very able boy, with a reputation for minimal attention, said that 'TASC week is the best thing in school. I wish I could work like this always'. Another child, talented in mechanical/technical problem-solving, yet who struggled academically, who, despite leaving our school a few years ago, makes what is becoming an annual pilgrimage to help with the activities, or at least to see what is happening, in TASC Week.

The pages that follow include lesson plans, photographs and evaluations of the eight challenges tackled so enthusiastically by both staff and children.

1. Social, Emotional and Spiritual: Prepare a reflection on creation.

2. Linguistic: Create a space/planet poem.

3. Mathematical: Create a 2D floor plan of a space station.

4. Scientific: Explore factors that could affect the launch of a rocket.

5. Mechanical/Technical: Design and make a rocket that will travel the furthest distance and survive!

6. Auditory/Musical: Create musical effects representing a planet of choice.

7. Physical/Movement: Create a sequence of movements conveying a space journey.

8. Visual/Spatial: Create a scene of a view from outer space and name it.

Social, Emotional and Spiritual: Prepare a reflection on creation

Learning Objectives	PoS	Cross curricular links
To respond sensitively, ask questions and prepare a reflection on creation		En 1a 2a 10 abc PSHE: 4f

Success Criteria:	Assessment Opportunities:
I can discuss my thoughts, opinions and questions sensitively with others I can work with others to present our group reflections to the class	Understanding of 'symbolism' Openness to abstract ideas
	Differentiation By outcome – very open-ended

Resources	Key Vocabulary	G&T
Bibles, Godly Play Script (with sequins + symbols + black card) Copies of Psalm 8: 'God the Creator' and poem: 'In the beginning'	Creation, sensitively, reflection, question, creator, faith, I wonder, universe, vastness of space	Awareness of spiritual ideas Understands symbolism
		SEN With teacher/peer support can think beyond the self
		EAL Has the language to express spiritual ideas

Delivery/Key Questions:		
Basic Thinking Skills spiritual, factual proof, non-proof belief, non-belief I wonder if --- I think that --- My opinion is --- I feel that ---	Advanced Thinking Skills Fact/opinion Compare, contrast Prioritise Imagine, create, invent	Useful Strategies Chart: fact/opinion Venn diagram: same, different Prioritise: tick chart

© Belle Wallace and Diana Cave 2007

	Activity:	
Gather and Organise	Refer to the 'Story of Creation' (link across the faiths). Brainstorm what we already know in words and pictures (use whiteboard). What does it tell us about God?	*What do I already know about this? Make links. Group ideas.*
Identify	To prepare a reflection on Creation using Godly Play Script. Tell the story of creation using 'I wonder' statements to enable reflection. Share with children two ideas from different sources – psalm 8 and creation poem by Steve Turner.	*What are we trying to do? How will we know if we have done well?*
Generate	Children to generate own ideas for presentation/reflection.	*How many ways can we do this? How can we find out?*
Decide	In small groups children discuss ideas and select best idea/idea to reflect on creation – own thoughts, opinions, questions ….	*Which way is best? Why? What should we do first?*
Implement	Children to practice expressing their ideas in any way they think appropriate and then refine (time limit).	*Is our plan working? Should we change anything?*
Evaluate		*Have we done it well? How could we do it better?*
Communicate	Presentation to whole group.	*Who can we tell about this? How can we show other people?*
Evaluate / Learn from Experience	Back to circle – children to feedback personal thoughts, etc., question one another, reflect together. A reflection of thoughts about the creation story: Underneath all the layers of our learning and our skills lies a heart that once knew how to marvel at the simple miracle of life – a heart that once received life without needing to conquer or control it, and a heart that can still recapture that first dawn of wonder …	*What have we learned to do? How else can we use this?*
Notes		

Social, Emotional and Spiritual: Prepare a reflection on creation

Things God made

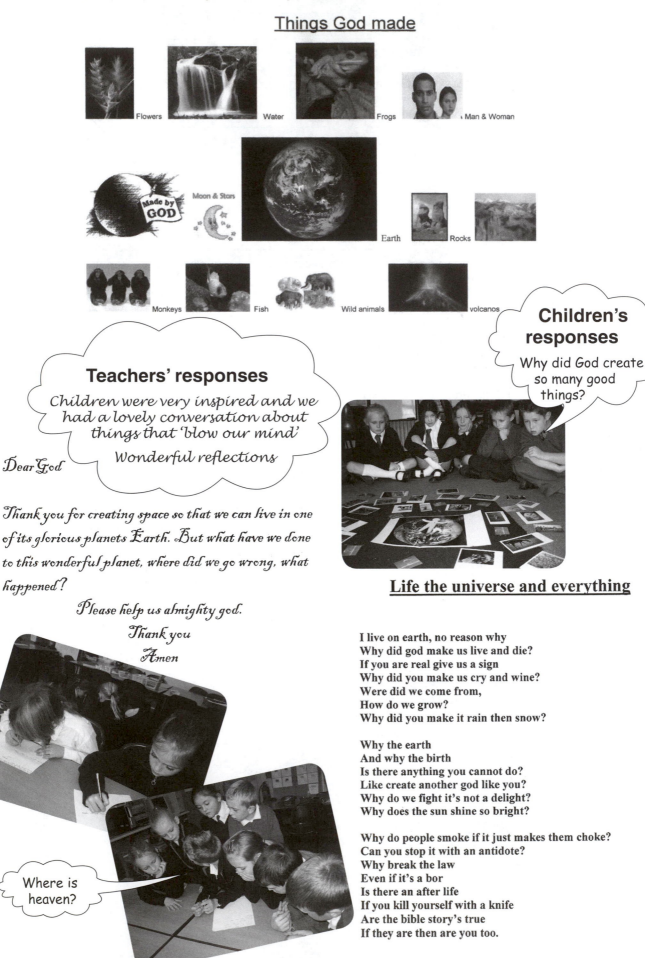

Flowers   Water   Frogs   Man & Woman

Made by GOD   Moon & Stars   Earth   Rocks

Monkeys   Fish   Wild animals   volcanos

Children's responses

Why did God create so many good things?

Teachers' responses

Children were very inspired and we had a lovely conversation about things that 'blow our mind'

Wonderful reflections

Dear God

Thank you for creating space so that we can live in one of its glorious planets Earth. But what have we done to this wonderful planet, where did we go wrong, what happened?

Please help us almighty god.

Thank you

Amen

Life the universe and everything

I live on earth, no reason why
Why did god make us live and die?
If you are real give us a sign
Why did you make us cry and wine?
Were did we come from,
How do we grow?
Why did you make it rain then snow?

Why the earth
And why the birth
Is there anything you cannot do?
Like create another god like you?
Why do we fight it's not a delight?
Why does the sun shine so bright?

Why do people smoke if it just makes them choke?
Can you stop it with an antidote?
Why break the law
Even if it's a bor
Is there an after life
If you kill yourself with a knife
Are the bible story's true
If they are then are you too.

Where is heaven?

Linguistic: Create a space/planet poem

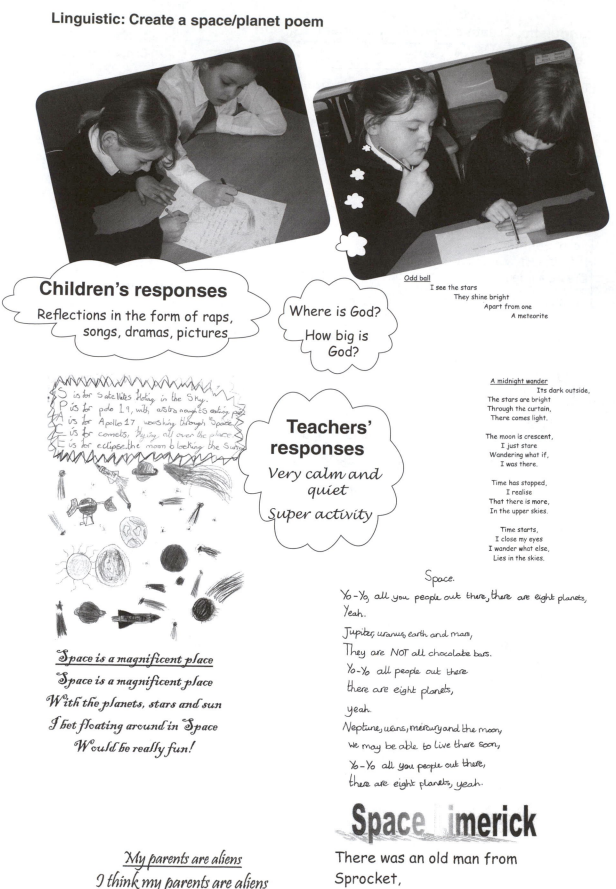

Children's responses

Reflections in the form of raps, songs, dramas, pictures

Where is God?

How big is God?

Odd ball
I see the stars
They shine bright
Apart from one
A meteorite

S is for Satellites floating in the Sky.
P is for pdo 19, with astronauts eating pie
A is for Apollo 17 wooshing through Space
C is for comets, flying all over the place
E is for eclipse the moon blocking the Sun

Teachers' responses

Very calm and quiet

Super activity

A midnight wander
Its dark outside,
The stars are bright
Through the curtain,
There comes light.

The moon is crescent,
I just stare
Wandering what if,
I was there.

Time has stopped,
I realise
That there is more,
In the upper skies.

Time starts,
I close my eyes
I wander what else,
Lies in the skies.

Space is a magnificent place
Space is a magnificent place
With the planets, stars and sun
I bet floating around in Space
Would be really fun!

Space.
Yo-Yo, all you people out there, there are eight planets,
Yeah.
Jupiter, uranus, earth and mars,
They are NOT all chocolate bars.
Yo-Yo all people out there
there are eight planets,
yeah.
Neptune, venus, mercury and the moon,
We may be able to live there soon,
Yo-Yo all you people out there,
there are eight planets, yeah.

Space Limerick

My parents are aliens
I think my parents are aliens
I'm serious, I think it's true!
Wait if my parents are aliens,
That makes me an alien too!

There was an old man from Sprocket,
Who went to the moon in a rocket,
He flew into a black hole,
Got swallowed up whole,
And now he's the size of my pocket.

Linguistic: Create a space/planet poem

Learning Objectives	PoS	Cross curricular links
To create a poem relating to space/planets, demonstrating knowledge of poetic forms	Enl 9a,10a En2 4afi,8cd En3 1de,7a	Sc4 Art

Success Criteria: **I can:** Identify different kinds of poems Create a poem using different forms of language	**Assessment Opportunities:** Use of poetic forms
	Differentiation By form, by outcome

Resources	Key Vocabulary	
Resources Range of space poems-from school library in a curver box	**Key Vocabulary** Space, planets, rhyme, rhythm, simile, metaphor, rap, personification, shape, figurative language, all parts of speech	**G&T** Uses advanced vocabulary and structures creatively
		SEN With teacher/peer support uses basic vocabulary imaginatively
		EAL Shows understanding in dual language

Delivery/Key Questions: What kinds of language do we find in the poems?	

Basic Thinking Skills	Advanced Thinking Skills	Useful Strategies
Basic Thinking Skills Parts of speech rhythm, rhyme simile, metaphor personification literal, figurative	**Advanced Thinking Skills** Extrapolate key words Classify and group Interpret and Create	**Useful Strategies** Thought showers Word maps Shape poems Illustrated poems

	Activity:	
Gather and Organise	Read a range of space poems-discuss poetic forms/ language used (as a class). Useful websites: www.google.co.uk put in '*space poems*'. www.shavick.com/andreapoemsspace.htm www.britishfestivalofspace.co.uk/spacecomp.htm www.bbc.co.uk/cbbc - put in 'space poems' on search, first result is *Write a Space Poem*.	*What do I already know about this?* *Make links. Group ideas.*
Identify	To create a poem relating to space/planets, demonstrating knowledge of poetic forms. Discuss success criteria.	*What are we trying to do?* *How will we know if we have done well?*
Generate	In pairs: think of subject, thought shower form for poem (rhyme, shape, rap, acrostic, simile, metaphor, nonsense, etc.)	*How many ways can we do this?* *How can we find out?*
Decide	Each pair to work on one idea i.e one poem for presentation – focus on figurative language.	*Which way is best? Why?* *What should we do first?*
Implement	During first lesson begin draft. Consider illustrations use poetry books for ideas.	*Is our plan working?* *Should we change anything?*
Evaluate	During second lesson proof-read, neat copy, practise performance.	*Have we done it well?* *How could we do it better?*
Communicate	Perform to class.	*Who can we tell about this?* *How can we show other people?*
Learn from Experience	Success criteria: We know a range of poetic forms.	*What have we learned to do?* *How else can we use this?*
Notes		

Mathematical: Create a 2D floor plan of a space station

Learning Objectives		PoS	Cross curricular links
To solve a given problem To use measuring skills of real life objects, i.e. people To create a 2D floor plan of a space station		Ma3	Science: Space; Life processes Geography: Keys English: Speaking and Listening
Success Criteria: **I can:** Use measurements accurately Scale measurements down Create a floor plan		**Assessment Opportunities:** Understands and can use the concept of scale	
		Differentiation Mixed abilities	
Resources A4 squared paper Crayons	**Key Vocabulary** Area, length, shape names, square, rectangle, quadrilateral.	**G&T** Conveys detail in design of complex layout in a floor plan	
		SEN With teacher/peer support can construct a simple floor plan	
		EAL Understands and can use the full range of basic thinking skills	
Delivery/Key Questions: How can we create a design of a space station?			
Basic Thinking Skills size, dimension length, breadth area shapes: square, rectangle, quadrilateral actual size, scale, scaled down	**Advanced Thinking Skills** Analyse complex needs Identify essential elements Synthesise a whole from parts Construct a scaled diagram	**Useful Strategies** Thought Showers Make a plan Colour code with a key	

	Activity:	
Gather and Organise	Discuss what a space station is. What do you need to live/ /exist for a length of time? Show pictures of Space Stations.	*What do I already know about this? Make links. Group ideas.*
Identify	Explain that they need to design a Space Station for 2 men and 2 women to survive in. Create success criteria. 1sq cm = 1 sq m.	*What are we trying to do? How will we know if we have done well?*
Generate	Discuss/note down room size + possible layout, power sources, scale of rooms etc.	*How many ways can we do this? How can we find out?*
Decide	Colours for key – which rooms, size of rooms, location of rooms.	*Which way is best? Why? What should we do first?*
Implement	In pairs, create and draw the floor plan on A4 squared paper (key on back).	*Is our plan working? Should we change anything?*
Evaluate	Evaluate against our success criteria created in Identify.	*Have we done it well? How could we do it better?*
Communicate	Show rest of the class and explain their designs and decision choices.	*Who can we tell about this? How can we show other people?*
Learn from Experience	Understand what we need to live – what's essential? Scale drawing, an awareness of size and dimensions. Understanding floor design.	*What have we learned to do? How else can we use this?*
Notes		

3. Mathematical: Create a 2D floor plan of a space station

4. Scientific: Explore factors that could affect the launch of a rocket

4. Scientific: Explore factors that could affect the launch of a rocket

Learning Objectives	PoS	Cross curricular links
To identify and explore variables which could affect the propulsion of a prototype rocket Set up 4 tables with equipment for exploring air pressure; water pressure; elastic band force and chemical change before the lesson	Sc1 1ab Sc1 2abcdefgijklm Sc3 1e; 2f Sc4 2bcde Sc4 4a	PSHE: 1abc 3efg 4a En1 1abcde En1 2abce En1 3abcdef Ma3 4abc DT: 1abcd

Success Criteria: I can: Predict what might happen Carry out an investigation Draw conclusions from experiments	Assessment Opportunities: Can identify variables which can affect propulsion
	Differentiation By outcome

Resources Video: Rocket launch. Rocket collection. Newspaper. Goggles, syringes, plastic tubing, vinegar, baking soda, elastic bands, washing up/pop bottles, film canisters	Key Vocabulary Variables, rockets, propel, propulsion, prototype, forces, air resistance, gravity, air pressure/pneumatics, water pressure/ hydraulics, elastic band force, chemical change/reaction, launch, trajectory, angle, streamlined, aerodynamics	G&T Identifies connections, collects data accurately, interprets evidence, sees cause and effect, generalises from all experiments
		SEN With teacher/peer support sees cause and effect in each experiment
		EAL Understands how to conduct an experiment, beginning to use technical language with understanding

Delivery/Key Questions: How do rockets move? What forces propel rockets?	

Basic Thinking Skills variable, constant resistance, propulsion pressure, pneumatics pressure, hydraulics launch, trajectory physical change, chemical change	Advanced Thinking Skills cause and effect compare, contrast, analyse, deduce prioritise, select organise data	Useful Strategies Flowchart sequence recording Diagrammatic recording

	Activity:	
Gather and Organise	Introduce the lesson by showing a video clip of a rocket launch. Review what was learned in the Space Centre workshops about rockets, planets, forces, air resistance and gravity. Demonstrate different means of propelling rockets: Air pressure; water pressure; elastic band force; chemical change.	*What do I already know about this?* *Make links. Group ideas.*
Identify	Explain that we are going to identify and explore variables which could affect the propulsion of a prototype rocket so that in the Mechanical/Technical challenge they will have the skills to build and launch a rocket. Negotiate success criteria.	*What are we trying to do?* *How will we know if we have done well?*
Generate	What factors/variables could have an effect on a successful school rocket launch? With Y3/4, you may like to direct attention to a range of equipment, asking, 'How could we use this?' What about fair testing?	*How many ways can we do this?* *How can we find out?*
Decide	Which means of propelling a simple rocket do you think will work best? Why? How shall we make a quick record of our findings? How are we going to avoid making a mess? How are we going to leave the table for the groups who follow us?	*Which way is best? Why?* *What should we do first?*
Implement	Divide the class between the 4 tables, explaining that they have only about 15 minutes at each table. Explore the means of propulsion at each table. Tidy and move on after about 15 minutes.	*Is our plan working? Should we change anything?*
Evaluate	As a group, discuss: Did we achieve the success criteria? Was our prediction accurate? Why? Why not? Which method worked best? Why? What are the limitations with each method?	*Have we done it well? How could we do it better?*
Communicate	Invite a spokesperson from each group to report on their findings.	*Who can we tell about this?* *How can we show other people?*
Learn from Experience	Ask the class to summarise what has been learned about: propelling rockets; working together. Consider other variables that could affect the success of a launch. (Rocket design; Launch trajectory, etc.) Where else might they find information before they attempt the Mech/Tech Rocket Launch Challenge?	*What have we learned to do?* *How else can we use this?*
Notes	Safety goggles?	

5. Mechanical/Technical: Design and make a rocket that will travel the furthest distance and survive!

Learning Objectives	PoS	Cross curricular links
To design and create a rocket that will travel the furthest distance and survive!	**1abcd** **2abcde** **3abc** **4abc** **5c**	PHSE 4a 10 En1 1ab En2 bc En3 acdf Ma3 1a 4b Sc4 2bcd

Success Criteria **I can:** Design and make a rocket and launch it successfully	Assessment Opportunities Transferred skills and technical skills
	Differentiation By outcome

Resources Plastic tubing, vinegar, baking soda, elastic bands, masking tape, glue, glue guns, card, cardboard tubes, washing up/ pop bottles, film canisters. Year Group Rocket Box (basic equipment only – will need to ask children to collect washing up/pop bottles, film canisters, cardboard tubes etc.)	Key Vocabulary Launch, trajectory, angle, projection, force, gravity, streamlined, aerodynamics, air resistance, hydraulic/pneumatic, chemical reaction	**G&T** Manipulates techniques confidently and creatively
		SEN With Teacher/peer support can make a simple rocket design
		EAL Understands and uses D/T skills

Delivery/Key Questions: How can we make a rocket that can be launched successfully?	

Basic Thinking Skills base, height, support, projectile power, launch balance, stability, efficiency angle, streamlined, projectile, aerodynamics physical, chemical reaction gravity, force	**Advanced Thinking Skills** Consider all factors Select and Organise Sequence steps Prototype and refinement	**Useful Strategies** **Discuss plans** **Sketch idea** **Test sections**

	Activity	
Gather and Organise	Science activity must be completed first. Website for NASA launch. What do we already know about aerodynamics, materials/joining materials?	*What do I already know about this? Make links. Group ideas.*
Identify	To create a rocket to be launched successfully. Explain that the distance travelled towards the target will be measured. What will make a successful launch?	*What are we trying to do? How will we know if we have done well?*
Generate	How could it be launched? (How will rocket fit into launch? Angle of trajectory?) Rocket styles?	*How many ways can we do this? How can we find out?*
Decide	Discuss options. Decide exactly what to do – create plan.	*Which way is best? Why? What should we do first?*
Implement	1 hr to make.	*Is our plan working? Should we change anything?*
Evaluate	How well did rocket meet the criteria? Test within class. What made a good rocket? etc Successful rocket from each class to compete in year group competition.	*Have we done it well? How could we do it better?*
Communicate	Report back to class – top tips for future rocketeers!	*Who can we tell about this? How can we show other people?*
Learn from Experience	Team work experience. Technical skills. Handling of materials.	*What have we learned to do? How else can we use this?*
Notes		

5. Mechanical/Technical: Design and make a rocket that will travel the furthest distance and survive!

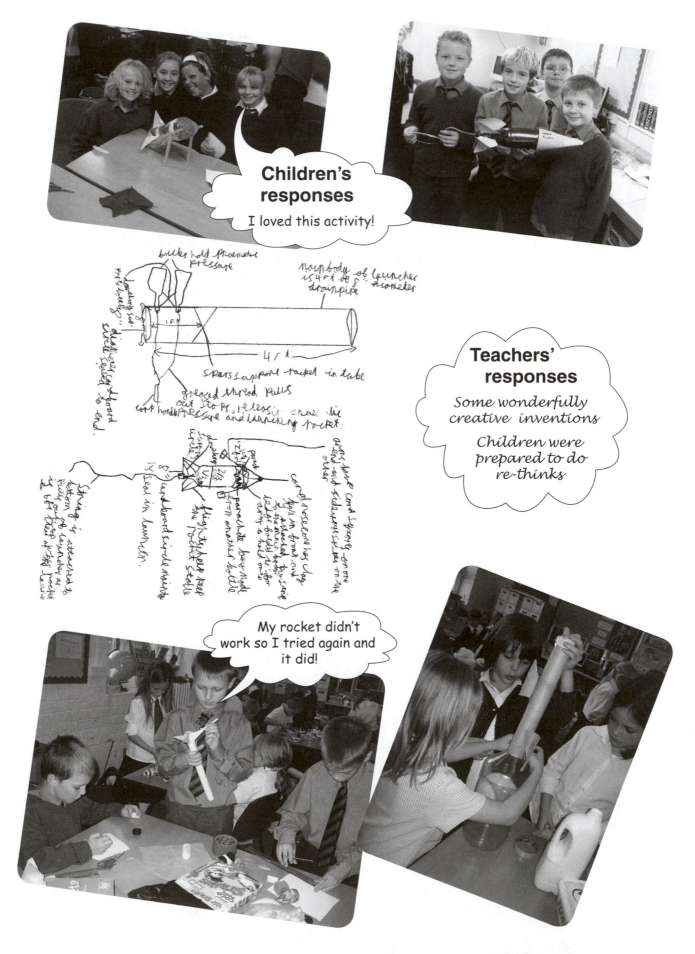

6. Auditory/Musical: Create musical effects representing a planet of choice

Children's responses

We worked well without arguing!

I really enjoyed the story of creation

Teachers' responses

Children enthralled by 'godly play'

Lovely free and creative sounds

Auditory/Musical: Create musical effects representing a planet of choice

Learning Objectives		PoS	Cross curricular links
To create effects representing a planet of choice		1bc 2b 3abc 4b 5c	English: Speaking and Listening Science: Sound ICT PSHE
Success Criteria: **I can:** Create a musical sequence to illustrate a planet I can use a variety of sounds to build a musical picture		\<col3+4 merged\>	**Assessment Opportunities:** Response to melody, rhythm and beat
			Differentiation Through outcome of group composition Mixed ability
Resources **Holst CD** **Ear-muffs for teachers!** **Pictures of planets** **Percussion** **Keyboards** **Recording equipment**	**Key Vocabulary** Tempo Timbre Dynamics Mood Texture Symphonic Poem		**G&T** Combines sounds, rhythm, and beat in creative ways
			SEN With Teacher/peer support can create a sequence of sounds
			EAL Can understand the technical words needed to interpret the task
Delivery/Key Questions: How can we create a musical picture that describes a planet?			
Basic Thinking Skills tempo, timbre, mood, musical texture symphonic poem rhythm, melody, beat	**Advanced Thinking Skills** Combine in new ways Synthesize Sequence and join smoothly		**Useful Strategies** Group discussion Tick-charts for evaluating Consider good points and revision points

	Activity:	
Gather and Organise	Name and discuss planets – view pictures and listen to Holst representation.	*What do I already know about this?* *Make links. Group ideas.*
Identify	To create a musical illustration of a chosen planet. Establish evaluation criteria.	*What are we trying to do?* *How will we know if we have done well?*
Generate	Discuss types of planet – mood it depicts/size/ volume/colour/timbre/tempo. Experiment with instruments.	*How many ways can we do this?* *How can we find out?*
Decide	Children decide on planet, instruments/voices, length of composition.	*Which way is best? Why?* *What should we do first?*
Implement	Children rehearse compositions and adapt ideas as necessary.	*Is our plan working?* *Should we change anything?*
Evaluate	Perform and record composition to class.	*Have we done it well?* *How could we do it better?*
Communicate	Listen back to recordings and evaluate compositions together as a class.	*Who can we tell about this?* *How can we show other people?*
Learn from experience	Discuss what they thought worked well. What would they change?	*What have we learned to do?* *How else can we use this?*
Notes		

7. Physical/Movement: Create a sequence of movements conveying a space journey

Learning Objectives	PoS	Cross curricular links
To create a sequence of movements conveying a space journey	**6abcd**	PSHE 4a Speaking/listening

Success Criteria: I can: Use different kinds of movements Create a sequence of movements to explain an idea	Assessment Opportunities: Accurate sense of space, speed, direction, shape Links movements sequentially
	Differentiation By outcome

Resources Space dance (extracts of CATS) Cassette Tape player	Key Vocabulary Step, turn, jump, travel, stillness, gesture, pathway, speed, level, floating, twisting, spiralling, zooming, creeping	G&T Fluent, seamless movements Imaginative interpretation
		SEN Beginning understanding of different kinds of movement Beginning to link movements
		EAL Can understand movement instructions

Delivery/Key Questions: What are the differences between movements on earth and movements in space?

Basic Thinking Skills full and half turn forwards, backwards clockwise, anti clockwise change direction higher, lower heavy, weightless individually, co-operatively	Advanced Thinking Skills Sequence, Order Compare, Contrast Practise and Refine Prioritise	Useful Strategies Think, Pair, Share Hitch-hike on to other ideas

	Activity:	
Gather and Organise	Discuss space journey – different stages and events. Play music – identify each section of music. 'Space Dance' 1. Preparing for space mission. Putting on space suit. (Fast – change of direction, fast moves and jumps. 2. Light, floating, turns, twists, change of level, weightlessness. 3. Land on moon/planet – creeping, low moves, exploring, sudden shocks, curious, facial expressions. 4. Spinning – fast turns, use of levels, partner spins. 5. Monsters – groups of 5/6. Move slowly.	*What do I already know about this?* *Make links. Group ideas.*
Identify	Create a sequence of movements for a journey into space. Work individually until end section where they create a group monster.	*What are we trying to do?* *How will we know if we have done well?*
Generate	Play music, allow children to generate movements to each section of the music. Pause at relevant intervals and share ideas. Discuss types of movement eg zooming, dashing, floating, creeping, spiralling.	*How many ways can we do this?* *How can we find out?*
Decide	Decide on individual preferred movements. In groups decide on monster sequence for last section of dance.	*Which way is best? Why?* *What should we do first?*
Implement	Play music for children to practise and refine. Work individually before coming together for monster in last section.	*Is our plan working?* *Should we change anything?*
Evaluate	Children to discuss with partner and share their progress and suggestions for improvement. Evaluate group monsters.	*Have we done it well?* *How could we do it better?*
Communicate	Perform to class	*Who can we tell about this?* *How can we show other people?*
Learn from experience	Feedback. Good ideas/movements. How could we improve this further?	*What have we learned to do?* *How else can we use this?*
Notes		

7. Physical/Movement: Create a sequence of movements conveying a space journey

Children's responses

I never thought I could do something like this!

Teachers' responses

The children worked very cooperatively without arguing!

The movements were fluid and expressive

I felt like I was really travelling in space

8. Visual/Spatial: Create a scene of a view from outer space and name it

Children's responses

I really enjoy thinking and creating for myself

Teachers' responses

We enjoyed imagining and reflecting on what God made - don't often get much of a chance to think about these things

Children listened attentively and their presentations varied and showed good understanding

I like to use colour in exciting ways

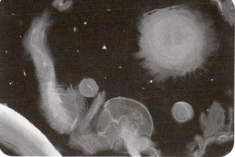

8. Visual/Spatial: Create a scene of a view from outer space and name it

Learning Objectives	PoS	Cross curricular links
Create a scene of a view from outer space and name it	1abc 2abc 3ab 4abc 5abc	English Science ICT Geography

Success Criteria: I can: Create an imaginary perspective in space Use a range of techniques creatively		Assessment Opportunities: Are the children able to use their imagination to create a view from space?
		Differentiation Paired responses

Resources Paper, card, magazines, fabric, texture gels, modroc, papier maché, paints, crayons, scissors, glue	Key Vocabulary Perspective, texture, view, reality, fantasy, tone, mood, contrasting, complementary colours, imagination	**G&T** Experiments confidently with techniques and methods Draws and paints with fine detail
		SEN With teacher/peer help can use basic techniques
		EAL Can understand and use a range of techniques

Delivery/Key Questions: How can we show an imaginary view from outer space?		

Basic Thinking Skills texture, mood distant, perspective reality, fantasy technique, effect	Advanced Thinking Skills Compare, contrast Analyse and synthesise Select and organise	Useful Strategies Sketches Technique trials

	Activity:	
Gather and Organise	Discuss what they imagine they could see: colours, textures, mood, shape, contrast between dark and light.	*What do I already know about this?* *Make links. Group ideas.*
Identify	Provide stimuli: PPT presentation. Create a scene of a view from outer space and name it. Discuss success criteria.	*What are we trying to do? How will we know if we have done well?*
Generate	Discuss in pairs their possible ideas. Will I use 2D/3D? Will it be a planet? What about perspective? (Close up/distance) What colours/materials will I use? Creatures? Will it be real or fantasy? Sketch and annotate 2–3 ideas.	*How many ways can we do this? How can we find out?*
Decide	Individually choose the best idea considering time, resources, effect you are trying to create. Make a list of resources they need to collect, if any. End of first session.	*Which way is best? Why? What should we do first?*
Implement	Produce view on paper, card, etc.	*Is our plan working? Should we change anything?*
Evaluate	Look at scene. Is it how you originally planned? Are you pleased with the result? What would you change?	*Have we done it well? How could we do it better?*
Communicate	Art walk. Discuss successful techniques.	*Who can we tell about this? How can we show other people?*
Learn from experience	Have I made good use of the time? Am I proud of my work? How do others view my work? Does it have a WOW factor?	*What have we learned to do? How else can we use this?*
Notes		

Conclusion

Undoubtedly, the full TASC weeks inspire and motivate both learners and teachers. But isolated TASC weeks on their own, without carry-over into the curriculum, are not enough to embed the TASC process in the minds of teachers and learners. Both teachers and learners need to refer to the TASC Framework as often as possible, so that it becomes a natural and autonomous process for 'thinking actively in a social context'. Every classroom has a TASC Wheel prominently displayed and teachers are encouraged to take every opportunity to use the whole TASC Framework for suitable activities or to use sections of the TASC Framework as appropriate. Planning for TASC activities is now part of our normal lesson planning. The children soon begin to refer to the TASC Wheel independently in their individual and group work. More able learners quickly internalise the TASC process and use it as their independent thinking guide for extended work; while other learners need to be reminded and helped – but they are able to use the TASC Framework to scaffold their thinking.

In conclusion, the following collections of comments reflect the responses of teachers and children to their TASC based work.

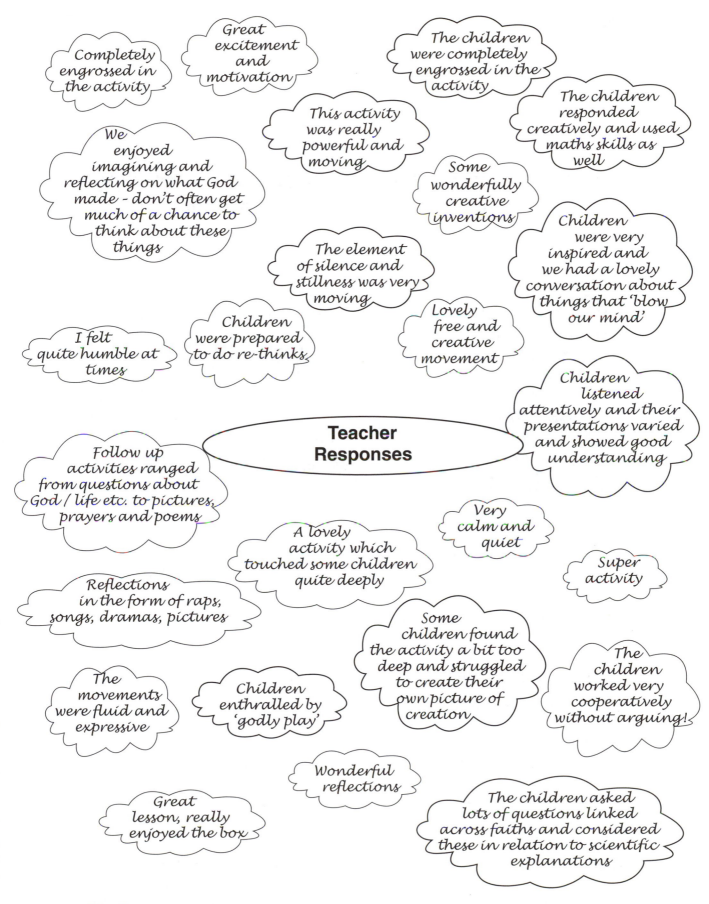

Completely engrossed in the activity

Great excitement and motivation

The children were completely engrossed in the activity

The children responded creatively and used maths skills as well

We enjoyed imagining and reflecting on what God made - don't often get much of a chance to think about these things

This activity was really powerful and moving

Some wonderfully creative inventions

Children were very inspired and we had a lovely conversation about things that 'blow our mind'

The element of silence and stillness was very moving

I felt quite humble at times

Children were prepared to do re-thinks

Lovely free and creative movement

Teacher Responses

Children listened attentively and their presentations varied and showed good understanding

Follow up activities ranged from questions about God / life etc. to pictures, prayers and poems

A lovely activity which touched some children quite deeply

Very calm and quiet

Super activity

Reflections in the form of raps, songs, dramas, pictures

Some children found the activity a bit too deep and struggled to create their own picture of creation

The children worked very cooperatively without arguing!

The movements were fluid and expressive

Children enthralled by 'godly play'

Wonderful reflections

Great lesson, really enjoyed the box

The children asked lots of questions linked across faiths and considered these in relation to scientific explanations

Reference

Wallace B. (in press) *A Tribute to Paulo Freire*.

Chapter 3

The children's voices

Research materials, book reviews and recording techniques for the TASC Project on Space and Rockets

The children of the National School, Grantham, Lincs

Photographs of co-authors

It might, at first, seem just a little unusual to include children as authors in a book for teachers! But we believe that learners know a great deal about teaching and learning! This is what we mean by 'pupil voice': they do know what they find interesting and what motivates them to sustain attention, effort and enjoyment. How often do we ask learners:

☐ Is my teaching meeting your learning needs?

☐ How can I do it better?

☐ Are the materials we are using really interesting?

☐ How do you feel about our lessons? Do you really enjoy them?

☐ Which lessons do you like the best? Why?

☐ Which lessons do you like the least? Why?

The children in the National CE Junior School have classes with very mixed abilities, including some very challenging pupils, which is a situation similar to many other schools across the country. But they are all very familiar with the TASC Framework, where they use it as the daily tool for guiding their thinking. Their enthusiastic response to becoming reviewers and to being

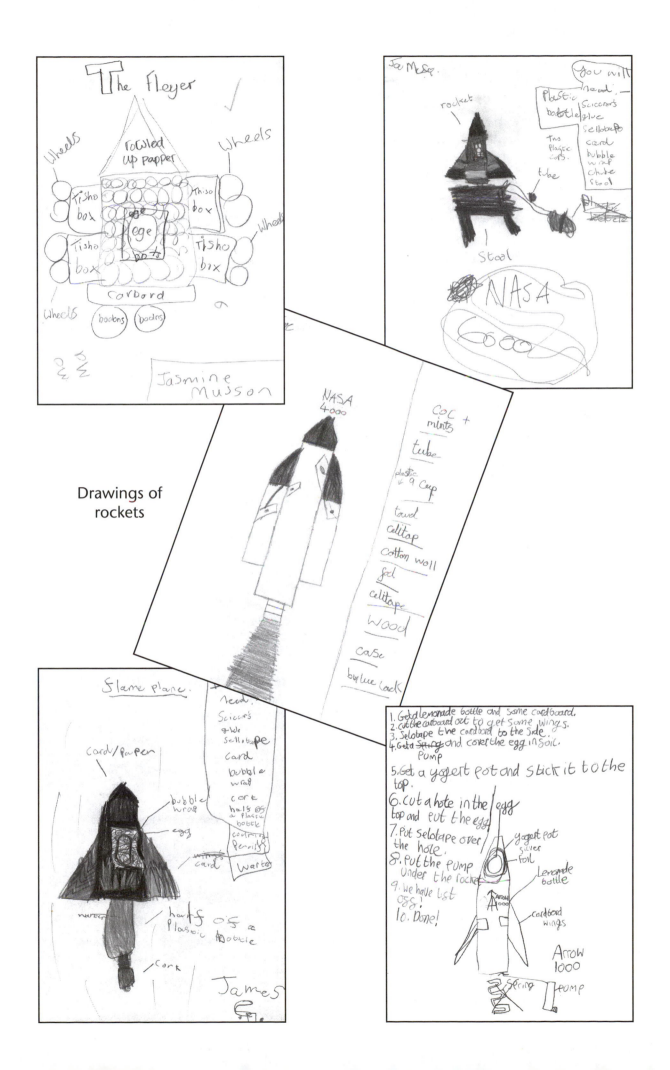

Drawings of rockets

published fired them with the determination to search out and review a wide range of interesting and useful classroom materials. They wanted to share their reviews with other children in other schools and were thrilled to be asked to do so. There was no problem with persisting with the effort of drafting and re-drafting because there was a real reason for persevering. They still remember the experience and have been looking forward to seeing their work in print.

We decided that since the book has a truly inclusive message then we could not exclude any pupil's review, so we have taken excerpts from each review that was written. What the reviews convey is that children are well capable of deciding what is interesting, relevant and exciting. They can make perceptive decisions about materials that they find both useful and inspiring and that listening to the pupils' voices is the first step in personalising learning and motivating children.

So, using the children's voice – here are their recommendations.

www.kidsastronomy.com
Review by Bobby Roberts

This is a good website It has games like crossword, hangman, memory games, shape match, sliding puzzles, word searches and quizzes. When you click on the planets it shows up lots of useful information, like what you'd weigh on a planet, what the planet and core look like, and how many moons it has. There is also space exploration where you are told about telescopes invented in the 17th century by Galileo. Before this, people thought the earth was encased in a giant sphere, and that stars were holes in it where the heavens seeped through above. ...

Today, we are no longer restricted to climbing mountains, we can actually leave the earth ... NASA's Shuttle Programme is one of the most exciting achievements in the world. ... Scientists dream of technologies that will allow us to travel through the many galaxies faster than the speed of light.

I really enjoyed reviewing this amazing website and recommend it to anyone researching astronomy.

www.kidsastronomy.com
Review by Lindsay Evans

This is a fascinating website – very enjoyable... and designed for kids. ... As well as being educational, there are lots of fun things to do ... there are 21 songs about Space and some movies to watch. ... It is a fun way to learn and the facts are amazing! ... If you think that learning about Space is boring, then you're absolutely wrong!

www.kidsastronomy.com
Review by Samuel Hyde

This website has a lot of good features, there are games, puzzles, colouring, jokes and information about stars and planets, black holes and quasars, galaxies and nebulas. ... Did you know that it takes Saturn 10.759.2 days to orbit the sun! The Fun Zone is the best part for me! ... I personally enjoy playing on a make-a-planet and star explorer. ... If you like star gazing, then you'll want to print off one of the many clear and simple sky maps. ...

www.astronomy.com
Review by Jake Samuel

We can learn a lot from websites, videos, books. ... But this website nearly tells you too much – for example, I learnt that our galaxy would take 13.6 billion years to get across – mmmm ... I wonder if they used a TASC Wheel? I think this website should get on everyone's favourite list.

www.space.com
Review by Jordan Taylor

This is an amazing site about space! It tells you about all different things like Earth, Mars, Venus, the Sun and Moon and many, many more! It shows you photos and facts and you can even play on this brilliant site! There is a discussion board, a job search and even a place where you can sign up! It also has clips that change every day and they are really good. ... There is also information on the NASA crew who go into space. It has an entertainment section where you can vote for the best space song ever! In the technology section there is a technology feature and also a search engine!

www.space.com
Review by Joe Rogers

This website is very attractive to young readers because it is specialised for kids and makes things clear. ... The diagrams and pictures help you to understand the text. The text has extremely good grammar so young ones can read it! It even has its own search bar!

www.nasa.gov
Review by Ambah Jackson-Keirle

To get on to this amazing website, go on to a Google search and type in NASA Space is so exciting! To me the most interesting part of this website is 'Beyond Rocketry'. ... You can get information about launching rockets and landing as well. I would like to work for NASA which means National

Aeronautics and Space Administration. ... you can get information on their business and they've got many sponsors.

www.bbc.co.uk/science/space/solar system
Review by Heather Walker

This site is suitable for children as it has puzzles to solve about the solar system, and easy to read explanations about Space. You can also quiz yourself about planets and watch video clips. If you click on different planets you can learn much more about them.

www.bbc.co.uk/science/space/solar system
Review by Hannah McDonald

I really enjoyed looking at the section on aliens as it has a map of famous UFO sightings around the world. Roswell is the most famous of them all. I think there's life in Space and there could be aliens. My knowledge of Space was very poor before I went on this website, but after a couple of days of research, I've discovered that Space is a wonderful exciting subject. ... As we have a telescope at home, I think I'd like to see what's really up in Space.

www.space.com
Review by Mia Wills

This website is full of information about what is happening in Space. It has many links such as Destinations, News, Space Flights, Technology, Science, Entertainment, Space Views, Night Skies and Community. For example, if you click on the link 'Science' it takes you to 'A Deep Hole found on Mars' or 'Loner Black Holes Lurk in Cosmic Voids'. It is a colourful and attractive website, and is easy to understand. The website also shows video clips that are very interesting.

www.yahoo.com
Review by Maddie Kirton

This is a responsible website for children over the age of 7 years. More than 2,000 bulleted facts are accompanied by hundreds of illustrations, diagrams and photographs. An extensive index allows you to find facts. The visual fact finder is very useful for personal needs. I especially like the museums like the London Natural History Museum.

www.spacecentre.co.uk
Review by Joseph Ryder

I have learnt what it takes to be a real astronaut – to be able to stand up to g-force 10 which is approximately 3 times an average roller coaster. Imagine some people are sick on a roller coaster! I also learnt to space walk, to use a toilet and to get used to eating dried food! One of the great things is the Rocket Tower which is a real life rocket and you can go all the way to the top rocket ... think of the height! ... it felt like you were travelling in space! Probably the greatest thing was the Space Theatre – it was brilliant!!!!!!!!!!!

Ewan McGregor talked you through what it was like to be an astronaut.

www.spacecentre.co.uk
Review by Sian Odell

The National Space Centre is a great place to learn about Space! ... My favourite activity is the weather forecast machine because you stand in a booth, read the words on a screen into a camera and a microphone ... moving your arms about trying to show where the weather is ... My least favourite place ... most definitely is the café where there is a giant rocket hanging above you when you're drinking a coke ... Believe me it isn't a nice feeling at all! The Simulator was another of my favourites ... We crashed through ice and zoomed to the planet Jupiter. ... It was scary but wonderful!

www.spacecentre.co.uk
Review by Charlotte Scorror

The National Space Centre was fantastic! It was co-founded by the University of Leicester ... Since then the Space Centre has put on amazing events with visits of famous people like Buzz Aldrin and Helen Sharman. The Space Theatre ... is shaped like a dome ... it made you feel as though you were in Space. The Rocket Tower is the famous symbol of the National Space Centre. It was a great day and if you do go there I hope you have a brilliant factual day out with the family!

www.spacecentre.co.uk
Review by Katie Carter and Anna Hodgetts

We recommend you to go to the National Space Centre, Leicester. There are 6 different galleries. In Gallery 1 you can see how different cultures thought the world was made. In another Gallery you can learn about the planets and comets. In another Gallery you can pretend to be an astronaut ... there is a Captain's chair and you have control! There is a gift shop where you can buy lots of things to do with Space. If you get hungry, there is a café. The Fun Factor is 10/10!

www.spacecentre.co.uk
Review by Michael Harrison and Josh Holmes

To learn about Space, you can go to the Science Museum in London and the Space Centre in Leicester. In 1961, Yuri Gagarin was the first man in Space, His spacecraft was called Vostok 1. The capsule orbited the earth at a speed of

27.000 kilometres per hour. The flight lasted 108 minutes. Yuri Gagarin was 327 kilometres from earth.

Space Game Halo 2 (X-box game)
Review by James Hall and Joseph Hopkins

This Space game is about two alien tribes who are enemies: each is trained until they are good enough to fight in the big war. ... There were only two aliens left – one of them got shot ... Buy this and find out how this very exciting game concluded with some extraordinary battle scenes and graphics ......

Hitchhiker's Guide to the Galaxy (film)
Review by Hannah Doughty

The film starts a few seconds before the nastiest creatures in the universe destroy earth. Arthur Dent is trying to defend his house because workmen want to make a bypass through it, but his best friend pulls him away and explains that the earth is about to be destroyed. Arthur and his friends hitchhike aboard the alien spacecraft and explore the universe with Trisha McMillan, a two headed galactic president, and Marvin, a paranoid android! I liked the humour in the film and it is also imaginative. It makes you think about all the hidden secrets that could be just around the corner for Earth. Don't Panic!

Apollo 13 (film)
Review by India Lloyd

I love this film because it makes me believe that one of the best things that could ever happen to me is to be a tourist in Space looking down at the earth, so minute and beautiful. ... I thought of reviewing this video because it has one of the best actors, Tom Hanks, and the Director Ron Howard is a superb director. ... It was very nerve wracking waiting for the pod to land in the sea. It made me cry a bit with happiness and relief that the men got back safely to their home, to Earth.

Illustrated Family Encyclopaedia
Review by Laura Bolshaw

I like this encyclopaedia because it was really easy to use, and I found out lots of information about Space travel. ... I thought it was good because I could see pictures of the people who first travelled In Space. Because I like animals ... I especially liked the picture of the chimpanzee in a space suit – it was really funny!

Zathura, A Space Adventure (film)
Review by Rebecca Ebb

It may have flaws, but I highly recommend this film if you like thrilling and exciting space adventures! ... I wanted to watch Zathura many times because as I got into the story, it got so tense, I nearly fell off the settee! Also, every minute made you wonder what would happen next. The special effects and terrific lighting help the film along the way. You also learn a lot about Space! In my school I asked 100 children if they enjoyed watching Zathura, and 85 said yes they did. Ten said that they wanted to watch it and 5 said it wasn't their kind of film ....

Space Travel by Interfact by Ian Graham
Software Twocan 1997
Review by Connor Brown

This book is a soft back that comes with a CDRom. My favourite chapters are: Man on the Moon, Rockets and Satellites. ... towards the back there is a glossary, this is especially good for children who haven't got a big vocabulary ... it explains the meanings of words like 'cosmonaut'. I thoroughly enjoyed reading this book ... I would recommend it to all my friends.

Eyewitness Astronomy Book by Kristen
Lippincott Dorling Kindersley 2004
Review by Lauren Ward

This book covers all the information you would want to know about Space. The word 'astronomy' comes from two Greek words: astron – meaning star, and nemien – meaning to name. The first chapter is about the study of the heavens; the next chapter is called 'Ancient Astronomy' and is about the cyclic motion of the sun, the moon and the stars. ... Another chapter tells you about astrology ... used by ancient priests and philosophers who believed that the movements of the stars had an effect on future events. ... I would recommend this book to all people who want to learn about Space ... you could learn a lot more than you already know ... I hope you enjoy reading this book.

Solar System by Ian Graham Collectafact 2000
Review by Laura Pigott

This book is quite informative and useful. Although the book is only small, it has thirteen sections all covering different topics. ... Did you know that the sun is a star? Did you know that the sun is about 5 billion years old? In about 5 billion years it will have grown 150 times its current size! ...

This book can be used for quick referencing, ... information and facts are clear and covered well. ...

It also has a 'true or false' section ... I found the glossary very useful as it is like a dictionary explaining main words ... even people who do not like reading would enjoy this book because it is only small. Sometimes people will not use a book if it is large because they think it may be boring.

Black Holes and Space and Uncle Albert by Russell Stannard Faber and Faber 2005
Review by Tobi Meuwissen

In the centre of the world there is something called Gravity! Gravity is something that keeps you on your feet when the earth is upside down to England, e.g. ... if you leave a wheelbarrow in the middle of your garden it will stay there. This is because of gravity pulling it towards the centre of the earth. This book is an amazing book because it explains everything clearly and you can understand it. The book brings some complicated ideas to life by using interesting characters ... Unfortunately, the most important [character] the beetle (which prefers to be called professor) is always getting things wrong ... I would thoroughly recommend this book to any age group from 9 – 90 years young!

Black Holes: And Other Oddities by Alex Barnett DK Publishing 2002
Review by Lucy Franklin and Bethany Gibson

This book inspired us with the good use of adjectives and the amazing pictures that catch your eye. ... Our favourite part is ... the introduction to black holes chapter. It says 'You're a big star'. You've burned fast and bright, then explode into a Supernova. After a blinding flash, most of you is scattered across the universe'. This book ... makes you understand that there is much, much more to space than you know. ... We hope you enjoy reading this book as much as we did.

The Universe: The Definitive Visual Guide Dorling Kindersley 2005
Review by Melissa Grainger

When reading this book, I noticed the amazing and wonderful pictures of space and the planets. But what I also liked was the vast amount of information included. Some of the text was hard for me to read because the book is aimed at older children and adults. I could tell, however, that it is a very accurate book because of the pictures and information. I liked the fact about the triple eclipse on Jupiter the most! Apparently, on the 28th of March 2004, three shadows were seen on Jupiter's surface because its three biggest moons passed between Jupiter and the sun!

The Marshall Children's Guide to Astronomy by Jacqueline Mitton Marshall Editions 1998
Review by Harry Murfin

... Stars are very, very hot balls of glowing gas, which shine with their own light. On a very dark night, you can see the light coming form billions of distant stars in our galaxy. We call it the Milky Way. ... Reading this book has encouraged me to pick up my telescope and sit outside with my family ... we all enjoy watching a lunar eclipse when you see the darkness of the earth's shadow creeping across the moon.

Avoid Being on Apollo 13! (Danger Zone) by Ian Graham Book House 2003
Review by Isabella Sterry

I picked this book because the introduction makes you feel that the book is referring to you, and if you want to be an astronaut it tells you how to prepare for the journey into Space. This book is eye-catching and I think it is aimed at children aged 8 to 11 because of the language used. The illustrations are witty so that children will take more notice of them. Overall I though it was a brilliant read, and I will read more books by Ian Graham.

Knowledge Masters Outer Space by Harry Ford and Kay Barnham Alligator Books Ltd 2005
Review by Ben Morrison

This is a non-fiction book about Space, complete with detailed diagrams, eye-catching illustrations and many fascinating facts. Each chapter covers different topics such as: 'What is a galaxy? 'Why do stars twinkle?' and 'How are stars formed?', and contains a summary and knowledge in 'question and answer' format. There are also interesting details on every page, including historical landmarks of our knowledge of space. The diagrams and text are usually simple, clear and easy to understand, but you can still learn new things. The book contains some complex scientific words that extend a young person's vocabulary and is aimed 8 to 12 year olds. I couldn't get my head out of this book because it was so interesting! Watch out for the other 11 books in the Knowledge Masters series because if they are good as this one, they will be worth reading.

Moon Landing, the race for the Moon by Carole Stott Dorling Kindersley 1999 and Moon Landing by Paul Mason Hachette Children's Books 2003
Reviews by Josh Kelham

In the book 'Moon Landing' by Carole Stott, I found the parts about the Apollo spacesuit, moon data, and out future on the moon most interesting. I especially enjoyed the section on scientific investigations ... my favourite invention is the robot explorer.

But 'Moon Landing 20th of July' by Paul Mason, is my favourite book because it has better pictures and more information. My favourite part is about when Neil Armstrong first stepped on the moon ...

If I could change something about the book, I would have a diagram of the rockets they launched. I would also like more information about Laika the space dog ... She lived in space for 10 days but then died in space. ...

Constellations of the Night Sky Dieppe Publishing Ltd.
Review by Matthew Broad

This is a non-fiction poster with 5 diagrams and 27 paragraphs. I like this product because the diagrams are simple and understandable and the information is bold and clear. The poster is colourful and attractive, and the colours help to explain some of the detail. I dislike some of the information, which is very technical and difficult to understand.

Space by Peter Bond Dorling Kindersley 1999
Review by Joseph Holmes

There are millions of things to learn in this book! For example, 'the edge of Olympus Mons is 4 km (2.4 miles)', and 'communication satellites are about 3 times longer than a car'. The quality of this book is very good – like the way it's laid out and the pictures. The way the information is put is really interesting. I would recommend this book for kids that are growing up.

The Usborne First Encyclopaedia of Space by Paul Dowswel Usborne Books 2001
Review by Fiona Standen

This is my older brother's book and a wonderful book to read! It contains lots of interesting and amazing facts about space with colourful and detailed pictures. ...

My favourite section is in the book is about Dangers and Disasters ... but the section needs less pictures and more writing because the balance is unequal and very little information is getting across to the reader. ... The book has over 40 website links ... my overall thoughts are that it is a great book for children.

The Encyclopaedia of Questions and Answers Paragon 2006
Review by Eleanor Dixon

The facts in this book are so detailed that you can actually imagine it happening in your head! ... it has an outstanding front cover and it has got a picture for every subject ... it has clear diagrams and cross-sections. ... It is a brilliant read, and I would recommend it to anyone interested in Space and like their information given in sharp bullet points.

Questions and Answers: Earth and Space by Anita Ganeri, John Malam, Clare Oliver and Adam Hibbert Paragon 2006
Review by Samuel McGurgan

Although I have read it from cover to cover, you can always refer back to it. It answers interesting questions like: Are we made of stardust? Yes, is the answer! Is it true that black holes turn you into spaghetti? Yes, the force of gravity would stretch and pull you apart. So you can see the book is quite funny! ... My opinion is that it is a great book, one to keep for my children and my grandchildren.

Interesting Facts about Space by Deanna Dumpleton

The phrase Milky Way comes from the band of white light that is visible from earth. It contains various stars ... it was discovered by Democritus, a Greek philosopher. The Milky Way has a whopping circumference of about 250–300 light years! ... there has been an estimate of about 400 billion stars!

Interesting Facts about Space by Daniel Gregory

The solar system is full of weird and wonderful things! That's why I want to be an astronaut! At the Big Bang the sun was born. As many rocks and meteorites hurtled through Space, earth and other planets were formed. The only planet with living creatures (that we know of) is earth.

Interesting Facts about Space by Leigh Broderick

Did you know:

that there is no wind in Space?

the sun is a huge ball of blazing gas?

our planet exists because it is just the right distance away from the sun for the water to be liquid and not ice or gas?

Interesting Facts about Space by Olivia Lloyd-Wickham

On June 30th 1971, tragedy struck. The ground team sent to greet the returning heroes opened the hatch of the spaceship to a terrible sight. The three men were dead. A valve had opened by mistake in Space and let all the air out of the ship. With no space suits to provide air, the cosmonauts died before reaching the ground.

BBC Science and nature: Space www.bbc.co.uk/ science/space
Review by Ross Hollingworth

Introduction

Hi to all you spacefans out there! I would like to tell you about a fantastic website that I have found. I have looked at lots of different ones but in my opinion this is the best. I will tell you why ...

On the space homepage you will find many interesting facts about space. There are many different sections to look at such as:
A 3D tour of the **Solar System**. You can click on any planet in the solar system such as Venus, Earth, Mars, etc and you will find lots of interesting information about each one.

One of the favourite things I liked in this section was reading about **Aliens and UFO's**.

Exploration looks at space travel. There is a picture of Doctor Who's Tardis in the Time Travel part which caught my eye.

Deep space is yet to be explored. Read all about the deadly black holes nick-named 'the hungry monsters of the Universe.

There is a part which looks at the **Origins and Mysteries** of the Universe: the past 15 billion years ago, the present, and predicts how it will all end in the future and much more.

The section on **Stars** tells you about the estimated 100 billion billion stars in the Universe, such as the birth and death of a star. It also tells you about why stars twinkle.

The **TV and Radio** section shows you links to TV and Radio programmes about space, such as Star Trek, Taken and the Hitchhikers' Guide to the Galaxy.

Now for the really fun part. I thought this was the best bit. The **Play Section** has Games, Quizzes, an Interactive space map and much more. There is a really good Solar System Jigsaw puzzle which was fun to do. I will be visiting Playspace again soon.

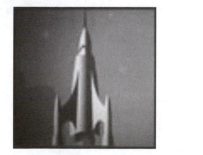 

On the **Message board** you can share your ideas, opinions, questions and answers.

Here are a few other links which you may want to visit which are also on this website:
The Sky at Night Online, Bright and Beautiful, Mars Travel Guide, and Mission Timeline.

The reasons I chose this website? The layout looks good and is simple to use. It is suitable for all ages, even my mum thought it was great! There is so much to see and do that you could re-visit it again and again. All the different games can be set for all ages and skills levels so that anyone can play and you can move on once you have completed a level. There are some great images of the planets in space to look at too.

I hope you take a look at this website and enjoy it as much as I did!

The Dorling Kindersley Picturepedia – SPACE
Review by Sophie Bell

This book is one volume of a set of books that gives information to young children on different topics. Together the books form a reference library of pictures and words giving basic knowledge for the young reader.

The book SPACE tells you all about the universe and space related topics, you can learn a lot about the subject by just looking at the pictures and reading the information.

I think it is a good book because it tells you about all sorts of facts, including the stars, the solar system and travelling into space. I particularly like the chapter about star constellations. It gives detailed images of the most well-known patterns, e.g. Leo – the leaping lion, Ursa Major – the great bear; and tells you where to see these in the sky. It tells you what to use to get a better view of the sky, e.g. binoculars and telescopes.

These are two other chapters I also enjoyed reading. They are about space stations and the rockets. I like these chapters because they tell me all about the rockets that were developed in the 1900's, from the first rocket to the later ones which carried people into space. In the space stations chapter they show you how the astronauts live in space.

Overall I think the book is good for the school age children that it is aimed at because it uses not just words but pictures too, so you can see what the things actually look like.

I would like to share some of my experimental Robots with you

Luke Michael Wren

I am in the process of compiling my own website: www.freewebs.com/lukedude30

I also used the following websites:
http://mindstorms.lego.com/NXTLOG/default.aspx – NXTLog. Part of the Lego site. NXT users post their projects here.

and

http://astolfo.com/home.asp – it is home page of Dave Astolfo, a member of the Mindstorms Developer Program. Includes details of a lot of robots, Both NXT and RCX.

These are some examples of my experimental Robots:

These are some of the skills we have learned to record our thinking

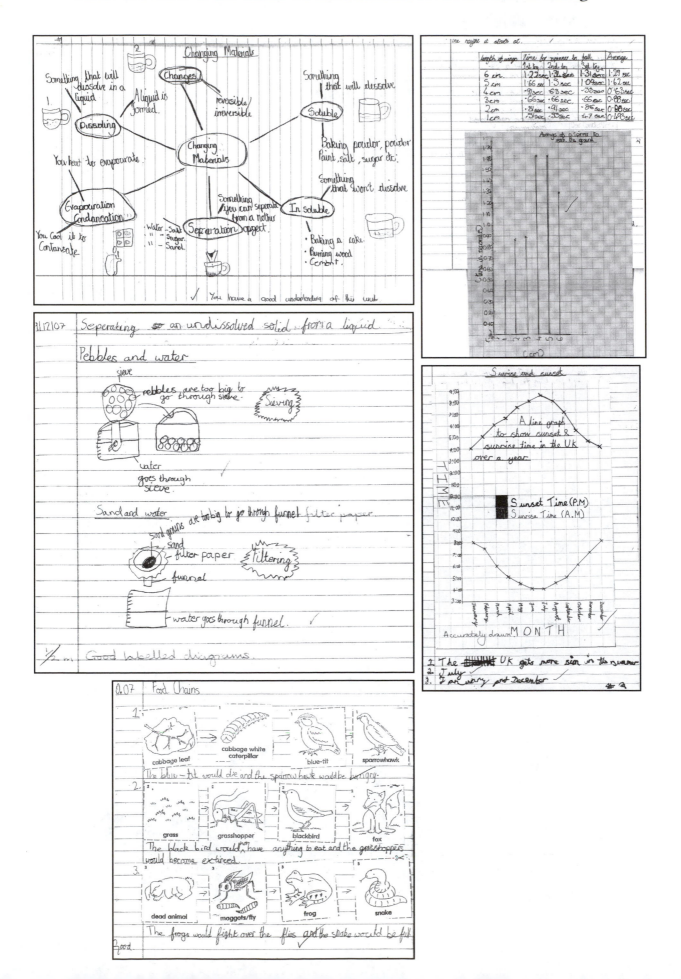

Who has the largest shin boys or girls?

Length in cm (y-axis: 0, 2, 4, 6, 8, 10, 12, 14, 16, 18, 20, 22, 24, 26, 28, 30)

Names (x-axis): Shakira, Heather, Emily, Olivia C, Lewis, Robbie, Joshua, Nicholas

I found out that girls have the largest shins.
I predicted that boys would have the largest shins.

■ girls
■ boys

My Habitat Investigation

Habitat	Prediction	organism found		features
wall	ants spiders ✓	Ants Spiders		Six legs invertebrate eight legs rate
trees	woodlice ants ✓	Ants		six legs invertebrate
nest	Birds ✓ chicks ✓	Birds Chicks		2 legs wings vertebrate
grass	ants lady bird ✓	Ants Ladybirds		six legs invertebrates
hedge	Lady bird ✓	Lady bird		wings six legs invertebrate
earth	worms ✓	worms Snail		saddle invertebrate
rocks	worms ✓	Worms Centipede		saddle legs
cracks	ants ✓	Ants		six legs invertebrate
benches	spiders ✓	spiders		8 legs invertebrate
Plants	lady bird ✓	Lady bird		6 legs wings invertebrate
well done.				

Materials

Solids — solids are very, very hard and could be dangerous.

Solids are very hard like metal and wood they are the exact opisite to

Liquids Liquids.

Gases

Some gases are poisenes

You can use gas masks to protect you from breathing in poisenes gases.

Liquid is a material like water it is the opisite to a solid.

You know some interesting things about solids, liquids and gases.

7.10.07

	9.00am	12.00
across	tree is 3m high Shadow is 2.9m long	Tree is 3m high Shadow is 1.5m long.
daytime the sun	3.00	6.00pm
	tree is 3m high. Shadow 2.9m long.	tree 3m high. Shadow 8.5m long.

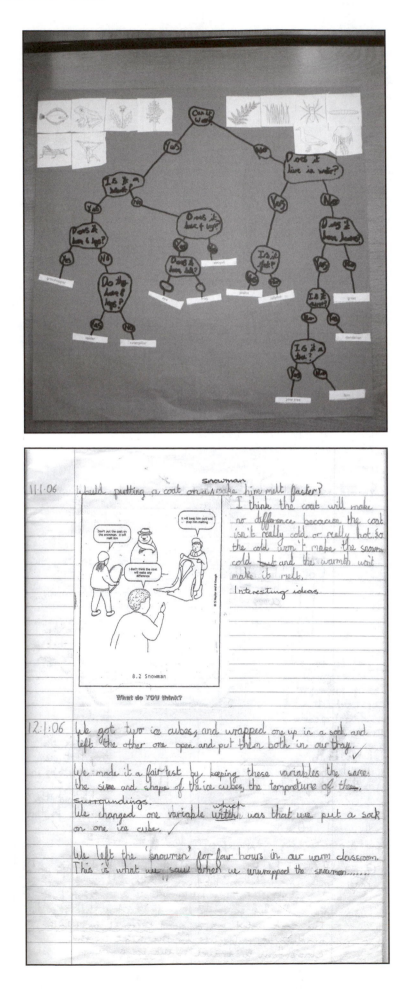

Our results

We put these pensils here to separate the ice cubes

This is the ice cube that we left in the open. ✓

This is the ice cube that was in the sock. ✓

This is the tray that we put everything in.

We put the ice cube in this sock.

Our Conclusion

Good ✓

Before I did this experiment, I thought that the coat would make no difference. But the sock kept the cold in. I learnt that putting something hot or cold in a container keeps the cold or hot in, so the thing would stay hot or cold. The sock acted as a good thermal insulator, making it difficult for the heat in the classroom to travel to the ice cube.

6.1.06 What will happen to hot and cold water left for 10 hours?

Super diagram ✓ m

We got two beakers and put hot water in one and cold icey water in. Then we put a temperature probe in each of them. The probes are connected to the data logger and the data logger is connected to the computer which shows us what the temperature is, by setting it out in a line graph, the cold water-blue line the hot water-red line, on the smart board. ✓

At the moment the red line is about 60°C. The blue line is just about 4°C ✓

After 10 hours I think that that the hot water will be quite high. Try to make predictions about both temperature readings with reasons.

Conclusion

We found out that the hot water fell to the temperature of the room, and the cold water rose for room temperature. ✓

Chapter 4

Examples of planning TASC science projects: Early Years and Key Stage 1

FunTASCit through Science: Years 1 and 2: Exploring forces

Example from Ollerton Primary School, Nottinghamshire

Headteacher: Carol Gilderdale

Class teachers: Lorraine Broadley, Helen Myatt-Smith, Jen Barthorpe, Helen Morrell, John Catling and Caroline Rafton.

Teaching Assistants: Wendy Whitby, Karen Young, Millie Papacoullas, Sue Reast, Janet Gibson, Jeanette Head, Janice Leatherland and Helen Lonsdale.

Planning across the curriculum

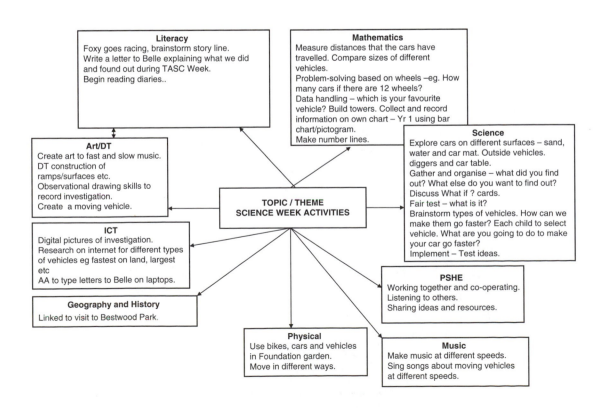

Literacy
Foxy goes racing, brainstorm story line.
Write a letter to Belle explaining what we did and found out during TASC Week.
Begin reading diaries..

Mathematics
Measure distances that the cars have travelled. Compare sizes of different vehicles.
Problem-solving based on wheels –eg. How many cars if there are 12 wheels?
Data handling – which is your favourite vehicle? Build towers. Collect and record information on own chart – Yr 1 using bar chart/pictogram.
Make number lines.

Art/DT
Create art to fast and slow music.
DT construction of ramps/surfaces etc.
Observational drawing skills to record investigation.
Create a moving vehicle.

Science
Explore cars on different surfaces – sand, water and car mat. Outside vehicles. diggers and car table.
Gather and organise – what did you find out? What else do you want to find out? Discuss What if ? cards.
Fair test – what is it?
Brainstorm types of vehicles. How can we make them go faster? Each child to select vehicle. What are you going to do to make your car go faster?
Implement – Test ideas.

ICT
Digital pictures of investigation.
Research on internet for different types of vehicles eg fastest on land, largest etc
AA to type letters to Belle on laptops.

TOPIC / THEME SCIENCE WEEK ACTIVITIES

Geography and History
Linked to visit to Bestwood Park.

PSHE
Working together and co-operating.
Listening to others.
Sharing ideas and resources.

Physical
Use bikes, cars and vehicles in Foundation garden.
Move in different ways.

Music
Make music at different speeds.
Sing songs about moving vehicles at different speeds.

Science Week objectives for Years 1 and 2

Science Objectives	TASC objectives
SC 1 Scientific Enquiry Investigative Skills 2a. Ask questions and decide how they might find answers 2b. Use first hand experience and simple info to answer questions 2d. Recognise when a test is fair 2g. Communicate what happened in a variety of ways 2j. Review their work and explain what they did SC 4 Physical processes Forces and Motion 2a. To find out about and describe the movement of familiar things 2b. That both pushes and pulls are examples of forces 2c. To recognise that when things speed up, slow down or change direction, there is a cause	To gather ideas from previous experiences To use and follow the TASC Wheel Processes To be able to think of own ways to develop the 'task' To be able to speak clearly to communicate findings To be able to co-operate with other children and share ideas To be able to evaluate and review the process

Ollerton Primary School has embedded the TASC Framework across the curriculum, identifying the basic skills the children need to develop and gradually leading the learners into using more advanced thinking skills and strategies. These TASC projects took place during a Science Week, but aspects of the science were still carried over into other curriculum areas. The teachers work in year groups to do the initial planning and preparation but the learners are encouraged to direct their own learning using the TASC Framework. Teaching assistants and parents support those pupils who need greater scaffolding, often doing the recording for them but encouraging the children to do the thinking.

Gather and Organise what we can say
about this vehicle

Generate ideas

Try out our ideas

Write how far our vehicle
can travel

Discuss what we have learned

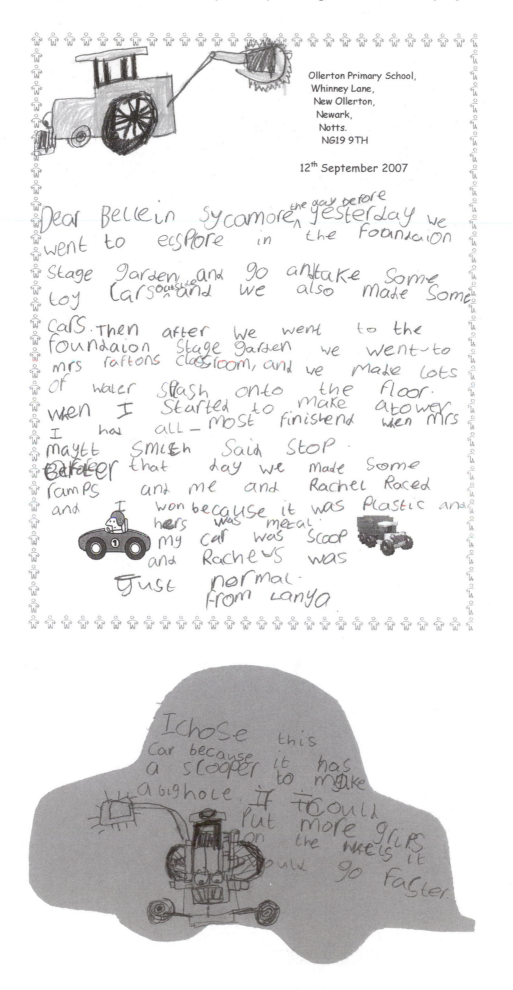

Ollerton Primary School,
Whinney Lane,
New Ollerton,
Newark,
Notts.
NG19 9TH

12th September 2007

Dear Bellein Sycamore, the day before yesterday we went to ecsplore in the Foundaion Stage garden and go anttake some toy Cars outside and we also made some cars. Then after we went to the Foundaion Stage garden we went to mrs raftons classroom, and we made lots of water splash onto the floor. when I started to make a tower I has all - most finishend when mrs maytt smith said stop. after that day we made some ramps and me and Rachel Raced and I won because it was Plastic and hers was metal. my car was scoop and Rachevs was just normal.

from Lanya

I chose this car because it has a scooper to make a big hole. If I could put more grips on the wheels it would go faster

Literacy
Narrative – A dark, dark tale.
Poetry – A hill is a house for an ant.
Labels and captions – linked to materials – parts of a house.
Narrative – Once upon a painting.

Numeracy
Blocks A and B
Counting/understanding number.
How many windows? bricks? chimneys. Odd/even numbers on houses.
Calculation – steps and stairs. Knowing & using number facts.
Understanding shape – 2d and 3D. shapes in the house – box modelling.

Science
Materials – Link to the house in the painting.
Identification of different materials, their properties and appropriateness for purpose.
Data handling about materials in their homes.
Healthy eating/harvest – What would have been harvested in the painting?

D&T
Using tools safely – preparing fruit salad.
Joining and fixing skills-box modelling – creating structures.
Preparing role play – Post Office.
Claywork – rolling, cutting and joining clay to make a tile pot house – Link to 3D work in Maths.

R.E
Belonging to our school, class, family, and church.
Christenings – visit to St Giles.
Harvest Festivals – celebrating a good harvest.

Geography
Developing a sense of our locality – types of building. Comparing Ollerton with New Ollerton – houses and size and type of shops. Jobs – link to the occupations in the painting.

Art
Colour mixing – stony shades – greys/browns Sketches of houses in the locality.
Fruit/vegetable/grain sketches (Harvest).
Sketching skills – different types of line – look at roof tile patterns.

Music
Recognising a variety of sounds – what sounds would they have heard in the old stone house? creaking doors/stone steps/crackling fire. – In the Hairy Scary Castle.
Making sounds with hands Identifying sound sources.
Different ways of playing instruments.

P.E.
Dance – country dancing – basic steps and actions – marching, clapping, skipping, finding a partner, swinging a partner, promenading.
Introducing a simple long dance – learning a sequence of actions.
Multisports.

Me and my world – The house at Het Steen (Reubens).

History
Old and new homes – developing a sense of the past – different materials used. Styles of building. Looking at household implements in the school Museum – Could these have been used at Het Steen?

I.C.T.
Skills based – switching on/off – computers/listening centres. Loading a programme from a desk-top icon.
Interactive games on IWB.

P.S.H.E.
Seal – New Beginnings.
Belonging, being part of a community, appreciating similarities and differences.
Self-awareness, managing feelings, understanding others' feelings, making choices.

FunTASCit through Science: Years 1 and 2: Me and my world

Example from Maun Infant and Nursery School, Nottinghamshire

Headteacher: Mary Haig

Class teachers and teaching assistants: Sally Pell, Rachel Fisher, Phil Somers, Rachel Otter, Anna Hadfield, Samantha Mason, Julie Westbury, Kerry Machant, Christine Taylor, Sarah Emmonds, Yvonne Fairhurst.

Planning the cross-curricular activities for two terms incorporating full TASC activities based on: Me and my world – the house at Het Steen (Reubens)

Maun Infants' School used the Reubens' picture to plan TASC learning activities across the curriculum and the children responded so well that the cross-curricular theme extended over two terms. Although the teachers plan the basic outline of activities ahead, such as visits, resources and mentors, the children are encouraged to direct their own learning activities by asking questions and following their own suggestions for activities. So the planning is flexible, since the children can initiate their own directions. The teachers ensure that the six areas of learning are covered.

☐ Personal, social and emotional development

☐ Communication, language and literacy

☐ Mathematical development

☐ Knowledge and understanding of the world

☐ Physical development

☐ Creative development.

The work planned incorporated Basic Thinking Skills, Recording skills, full TASC activities and activities that used sections of the TASC Framework as appropriate.

Medium Term Planning

Theme: An Autumn Landscape with a view of Het Steen in the early morning   **Year group: ONE**   **Term: Summer 2007**

Focus	Induction		Shire horses		Farming and markets	
Subject	One 16-4-07	Two 23-4-07	Three 30-4-07	Four 7-5-07	Five 14-5-07	Six 21-5-07
Literacy	In the painting I can see … Sentence revision	Narrative Once Upon a Painting	Recount – visit to the horse. Identify animals in the painting – non-fiction work about cows, horses and dogs. Questions Why, when, where, how, etc.		Farming and markets – 'Farmer Duck'	Farming and markets - poetry
Numeracy	Addition	Ordering numbers	Measures – length (hands – link to horse visit). Measures – capacity – yoghurt pots, jugs, litre containers, buckets. Measuring food for 'Winston'.		TASC Problem solving Design and make a nosebag for a horse. How much food will it hold? – use different containers to measure. Record results in a simple chart.	Money – counting in 5s, 10s
Science **LO** Animals Growing Plants Sound & hearing	To be able to identify a range of animals (including humans) and know the names of the young. To be able to identify the different parts of an animal. To understand how and why animals are used on a farm. To begin to understand the ideal conditions for looking after a range of animals (maths link). To be able to collate information into a simple table. NB: INCUBATOR IN F2 UNIT					
activity			Children to identify the different animals they can see in the painting and decide which they want to learn more about.	Visit to see the shire horse pulling logs in the forest. Compare the work of the shire horse with the horses in the painting. Draw and label a picture of a horse (pre-visit). Repeat activity after visit and compare.	Discuss why the horse was used on the farm. Why are other animals reared on farms? Sort animals found on a farm into categories of pets and/or working animals.	Use 'Animality' book Identify animals Habitats Match adults to young Life cycles Food, etc.
ICT **LO** Labelling and classifying Using a graphing package	To know how to shut down a PC.	To begin to understand the layout of the keyboard.		To be able to use capital letters and a full stop when word processing.	To be able to position themselves effectively to use the IWB. ICT link	To be able to program a programmable toy to follow a simple route. To be able to record a simple route for others to follow.
activity	Revision from previous term.	Type name and change font styles. Signing in the morning – use of Shift, space bar and enter key.		Redrafting writing about the shire horse visit.	Pets Graph Using the Black Cat graphing package. Children collect information on a simple chart then transfer onto a graph on the computer. ICT link. Maths base – children to use the program independently.	Use Beebots to travel to different areas of the painting
RE **LO** Creation stories and respect for the environment and other people	To listen to and respond to stories from the bible. To be able to retell significant parts of the stories they have heard from the bible. To understand that the bible is a special book for Christians.					

activity	Revisit the bible as a special book for Christians and read the first part of the Creation story – Darkness and Light.	Continue with the story of the creation. Children to record in their own creation book. Sky/Heaven	Continue with the story of the creation. Children to record in their own creation book. – land/ water/plants	Continue with the story of the creation. Children to record in their own creation book. Moon and stars/Sun	Continue with the story of the creation. Children to record in their own creation book. Birds and fish
DT LO Structures	To be able to use a small construction kit to create a model.	To be able to build a model following simple instructions and plans. TASC Activity.	To be able to create a model from reclaimed materials. To be able to select and use joining techniques and resources appropriately. To be able to draw a model and name its parts. To be able to use tools sensibly and safely.		
activity	Using small Lego and/or building bricks, recreate the house in the painting.	Making 'stand up' horse cards for display of shire horse work – following instructions and observing modelling by teacher. TASC activity.	Making farm animals, farm buildings and vehicles from junk modelling materials. Drawing and labelling their completed models. Making farm animals out of clay/plasticine/ dough.		
History LO	To be able to identify old and new objects and talk about some things people did long ago and what they do now.	To be able to talk about the differences between old and new objects and how people lived in the past and how they do now.			
activity	Look at the painting and work out how we can guess why it was painted some time ago.	Follow up to Shire horse visit – farming methods and how they have changed.	Look at methods of transport in the painting and compare to transport of modern day.		
Geography LO Our local environment	To be able to talk about where something is in a place.	To be able to describe the basic features of a place. To be able to talk about the differences between 2 places. To understand that a map is a record of features in the environment. To be able to recognise some of the features recorded on a map. To be able to record some of the features they have observed on a journey.			
activity	Looking at the painting and introduce vocabulary of distance, foreground, between, next to, across from, above, below, foreground.	Discussing and listing features in the painting-stream, bridge, fields, path, forest. Labelling a picture. Looking at similarities/differences in the painting and our view from the playground. Making a visual/3D map of the Painting and of our journey to Boughton Brake. Drawing simple plans which include some of the features they saw on their journey to see the shire horses.			
Art LO Printing, Texture and Pattern	To be able to mix colours from a limited palette.	To record from first hand observation.	To experiment with clay, changing the shape of objects by adding to them or taking clay away. To work as part of a group to create an artefact. TASC activity.	To look at how other artists have used paint or colour and respond to this.	
activity	Children to identify what colours they can see in the painting, then using powder paint to mix shades.	Working from colours found in the painting – mix shades using pastels. (Children wanted blue, green, brown.)	Pencil sketches of horses during visit and working from photographs back at school.	Sculpting/moulding farm animals. Adding fine detail with tools, joining legs with slip. Working with a partner to design and make a nose bag for a shire horse. Working alongside ceramicist to create a mosaic	Discuss life and works of Rubens' paintings, his home. Can they paint their home and garden?

Music LO Exploring pitch, timbre, tempo and dynamics.	To be able to sing in unison.	To understand what is meant by pitch.	To know how to control the pitch of their voice. To respond to changes in pitch.	To respond to changes in pitch. To relate sounds to symbols.	To relate sounds to symbols.
activity	Revise songs learnt since September.	Listen to and sing 5 Little Froggies track 42, indicating with hand up, down and to and fro. Use high, medium and low voices to say 3 bears rap. Show pictures of 3 bears and sing a nursery rhyme in appropriate voice.	Sing Slide song track 43 to practice moving pitch. Crouch low, rising little by little to full height then slide to the floor at the end. Play Jacks game track 44 Can they indicate with their hands if music is going up down or staying the same? Listen to Miss Mary Mac track 45. Does it go up/down stay the same? Does it jump or move by step. Children use hands to indicate pitch movement.	Play Jack's game responding to pitch, changes with movement – this time using a Xylophone (hidden). Sing Miss Mary Mac – match the way pitch moves with whole body actions. Listen to Playful Pizzicato to recognise high and low pitch tracks 46-48, discuss, then children match movements to the pitch of the music.	Listen to hot cross buns and draw the melody in the air track 49. Play Pease Pudding Hot. Draw melody in the air.

PE GAMES Large ball skills and games

To know and show different ways of using a ball. Based on Val Sabin SOW
To understand how to use apparatus for its intended purpose.
To observe, copy and play games as an individual and in two's.
To move safely and actively about the space.

activity	Lesson 1 (outside)	Lesson 2	Lesson 3	Lesson 4	Lesson 5	Lesson 6
	Warm up – jogging round field. **Main** – sending a ball in various ways to a partner and ensuring they get in line to send/receive the ball.	*build on previous week's session to consolidate skills* **Warm up** – jogging **Main** – sending a ball in various ways to a partner and ensuring they get in line to send/receive the ball.	**Warm up** *jogging stopping to a signal.* **Main** Individual – looking for different ways of sending and retrieving a ball. Then working with a partner to practise these skills	**Warm up** *Jogging, avoiding contact, stopping under control* **Main** Moving the ball along the ground but keeping it close to the body, using feet, hands. Holding the ball with different parts of the body. Rolling the ball and retrieving.	**Warm up** *Walking in different directions, forwards backwards, sideways.* **Main** Throwing and catching – stationary and on the move. Bouncing and catching the ball –stationary. Continual bouncing on the move. In pairs, aim and bounce the ball so that it reaches your partner.	**Warm up** *Running in and out of spaces stop and touch the floor.* **Main** throwing and catching small apparatus – 2 hands and 1 hand. Bounce the ball and catch with 2 hands. Pat the ball downwards and keep it bouncing. Throw ball in the air let it bounce and then catch it.

		Lesson 1	Lesson 2	Lesson 3	Lesson 4	Lesson 5
PE GYM Rocking and rolling	To spin, rock, turn and roll with control on various parts of the body. Based on Val Sabin SOW To plan and link a series of movements together. To work safely with an awareness of others. To adapt work from the floor safely onto apparatus.					
activity		**Warm up** *Stretching and mobilising joints* **Main** Floor work. Can they rise from a sitting position to standing without putting their hands on the floor? Rock backwards and forwards to make it easier. Rocking on other parts of the body. Practice moving around on a signal, stop and roll.	**Warm up** *Stretching and mobilising joints* **Main** Floor work. Rocking on different parts of the body. Practice moving around on a signal, stop and roll. Making curved shapes with body-rolls. Rolling with a stretched body. Place mats around the hall. Children to move around the hall, when they arrive at a mat, stop and roll.	**Warm up** *Stretching and mobilising joints* **Main** Floor work. Place mats around the hall. Children to move around the hall, when they arrive at a mat, stop and roll. **Apparatus** Moving along the benches, spring, landing on feet then roll.	**Warm up** *Stretching and mobilising joints* **Main** Floor work. Pencil rolls – stretched arms, pointed toes, from back to tummy and back again. Rolling sideways in a curled shape. Rock, then roll slowly and quickly.	**Warm up** *Stretching and mobilising joints* **Main** Floor work. On mats curl up tightly and roll over smoothly to land as you started. Benches – Finding different ways to travel over/under/ along and around. Moving from a curled up roll to a stretched out roll.
DRAMA LO		Drama session planned and taught by Anne Readman.	To be able to share ideas and negotiate roles.	Drama session planned and taught by Anne Readman.	Creating freeze frames of different areas of the painting.	Drama session planned and taught by Anne Readman.
activity		To be able to share ideas and negotiate roles. Look at the painting – type of drama activities could we do from it?	Revisit week 1 ideas and begin to work out a sequence of activities.		Conversations on the horse and cart.	
PSHE LO		To be able to work as a team.	To know how to keep safe when out on an educational visit.	To be able to negotiate and share ideas.	To know what makes a good speaker and a good listener.	
activity		Parachute activities.	Visit to Boughton Brake to watch shire horse pulling logs.	Set a new class target.	Voices activities and circle games.	

Focus	Trees			Birds and skyscapes			
Subject	Seven 4-6-07	Eight 11-6-07	Nine 18-6-07	Ten 25-6-07	Eleven 2-7-07	Twelve 9-7-07	Thirteen 16-7-07
Literacy	Information text – trees in the school grounds.	Trees – poetry.	Trees – visit to Boughton Brake – recount.	Non-fiction – birds.	Narrative –Wind Hover.	Narrative – Chicken Licken	
Numeracy	Shape symmetry	Odd/even numbers to 20. Investigation.	Measuring – link to TASC activities.	Addition, subtraction – repeated addition.	Handling data – bird count, etc.	Problem solving	
Science LO	To be able to identify the different parts of a plant/tree. To know the ideal conditions for growth. To be able to identify some of the plants found in the painting.			To be able to do accurate observational drawings to identify different body parts of a bird. To know the life cycle of a bird.	To be able to make observations of sounds by listening carefully. To understand we can make sound in a variety of ways. To recognise that when objects generate sounds something moves or vibrates.		
activity	Lessons 1&2	Lesson 3	Lesson 4 Lesson 5	Work with bird artist and do follow up drawings from photos.	Look at the different instruments and see what happens when rice grains are put on top of a drum, and what happens to strings on a guitar, etc. Make different sound effects using instruments and parts of the body to accompany the Windhover story. TASC activity. Music link.		
ICT LO	To be able to programme a programmable toy to follow a simple route.		To be able to record a simple route for others to follow. To be able to use a paint package.		To be able to use the keyboard to write a simple sentence independently.		
activity	Use Beebots to travel to different areas of the painting.		Build structures and write route out using arrows and numbers to show directions and number of key presses required. Use fresco programme to produce a representation of either a leaf or a tree.		Write a simple sentence or sentences about a bird or birds.		
RE LO	To understand what is involved on effective listening. To listen and respond to others.		To take part in setting ground rules for the playground.	To develop skills of discussion, negotiation and co-operation in a group. To take turns in discussion and take views of others into account.		To express opinions about real life issues. To recognise that there can be conflicting views and a need to compromise.	
activity	Model talking to another adult with the listener demonstrating poor listening. What did the children see the listener do wrong – list what should they have done.		Look at the school rule – how could we apply this at playtime? Take camera out at playtime to try to capture evidence of this for display.	In mixed ability groups children to decide one person to be in charge and report back to rest of class, one person to be the observer to report back on any good listening observed. Give one piece of playground equipment. Can they devise 3 rules for safe use?		Draw/write activity about eating lunch in the hall – which aspects they like/dislike. Discuss how we could improve the experience.	

DT **LO**	To be able to create a design. To be able to sew a design. To be able to thread a needle.	To be able to design and make a 3D model using a variety of cutting and joining techniques. TASC activity.				
activity	Sewing leaves – **red** spots. Sewing trees – **orange** spots. Making felt – **green** spots.	Sew sock 'grass heads'. Turn into scarecrows.	**TASC activity.** Use shoeboxes to create a wagon for the model horse – paired activity. Scarecrow making day – with parents.			
History **LO**	To know that people live in different types of home. To be able to use appropriate vocabulary to talk about homes. To recognise common external features of domestic dwellings.	To identify key features of a home built a long time ago. To be able to identify differences between 2 homes built at different times.	To recognise different rooms and household objects from long ago. To be able to describe characteristics of household objects from long ago. To know how to answer questions about household objects from long ago.			
activity	Look at photographs of different types of dwelling. Which are like their own? How are others different? Label different types of homes. Walk to look at homes near school – recognising common features and materials used.	Look at photographs of older dwellings – including Het Steen and discuss how these homes are different to modern homes – materials/windows/ doors, etc.	Look at 'Peepo' – identify rooms and notice differences with regard to furniture/appliances. Look at household objects from school Museum. What questions would they like to ask? Discuss uses of objects.			
Geography **LO**	To know their address and that they travel to school To develop a sense of place in relation to home and school. To be able to describe a route.	To be able to recognise some of the physical and human features of the locality. To understand the ways in which these features are used.	To be able to describe features of the local environment. To express views about those features. To understand that changes occur to their environment.			
activity	Writing their addresses – explain what each line in their address signifies. Locating their home on a street map. Discuss who lives nearest to/furthest from school. Survey of how they travel to school. Drawing route from home to school.	Look at photographs of locality. Identify what individual buildings are used for. Sort into homes/business/leisure. Place them in location to school.	Walk around locality to identify features and any changes that are occurring. Sort photographs of attractive and unattractive places. Looking at different buildings – what jobs might exist?			
Art **LO**	To use natural objects as a medium for printing.	To use the form and structure of a leaf to create a printing block.	To record from first hand observation patterns found in the natural world.	To look at how other artists have applied and used paint or colour.	To use watercolours to create a picture.	To create artefacts as part of a group. TASC activity.
activity	Leaf printing	Making string printing blocks. Using Polyprint to create a printing block.	Sketches and rubbings of trees.	Working alongside Bird artist – Michael Warren.	Watercolour pictures of birds. TASC activity.	Working alongside Comprehensive pupils – bird-making. TASC activity.

Music	To identify classroom instruments and know how their sounds can be changed.	To identify classroom instruments and know how their sounds can be changed.	To identify different ways instruments make sounds. To identify that sounds can be represented by symbols.	To know how symbols can be used to describe changing sounds. To listen carefully and respond to sounds using movement.	To listen carefully and respond to sounds using movement. To compose a class composition and contribute towards a class score.	To compose a class composition and create a class score. TASC activity.
activity	Sing I am the music man. Track 1 to practice playing instruments. Sing Bang, Bang track 2, the sticks go bang to explore volume. Track 3 Identifying instruments by their sound.	Sing track 5 I can see coconuts and choose instruments to accompany. Listen to track 2, Slowly, slowly and explore playing slowly and quickly Listen to track 3 Rainforest music to identify volume.	Use Coconuts score to match notation with sound. Sing when you play the tambour track 8 to explore graphic symbols. Sing jenny, tap the sticks track 9 to revise playing instruments loudly and quietly.	Sing Jenny, Tap the Sticks responding to symbols track 10 and decide on symbols to represent loudly/quietly. Sing Silence and Sound track 11 and 12 responding to graphic symbols. Listen to Rainforest music and match volume to symbols and movement. Track 7.	Sing Yo, Ho, Ho and make footstep sounds Track 13. Discuss sound and notation for each of the island scenes. Notate music for the island scenes.	TASC activity. Play a game to complete a score of treasure island music. Rehearse a performance. Perform and record. TASC activity.
PE games Ball skills and skipping	To be able to steer and send a ball safely in different directions using a bat. To be able to skip with a rope. To be able to change the rules of a game to make it better or more challenging. To understand the importance of 'rules' when playing with a bat.				**Based on Val Sabin SOW**	
activity	**Lesson 1** Notes made on lesson plans.	**Lesson 2** Notes made on lesson plans.	**Lesson 3** Notes made on lesson plans.	**Lesson 4** Notes made on lesson plans.	**Lesson 4** Notes made on lesson plans. Carried forward.	**Lesson 5** Notes made on lesson plans. **Fun Sports Day**
PE dance	To be able to perform a range of movements suitable to the idea. To be able to change and vary directions and speeds. To be able to improvise an idea. To be able to link 2 or 3 dance movements together.					

activity	Revise movements from country dance module.	Work individually to practice linking 2 movements – 1 fast and 1 slow.	Work individually to practice linking 2 movements together – 1 high and 1 low.	Carried forward from previous week.			
DRAMA		To be able to work with a group and exchange ideas.		Drama session planned and taught by Anne Readman.	Session carried forward.		
activity		In small groups create people from the painting and prepare for a walk.	The council want to build on Boughton Brake – what can the children do about it? Teacher in role as lead member of council. Some children as council members for the idea and others as residents against it.	To be able to work with others and exchange ideas.	Drama session planned and taught by Anne Readman.	Session carried forward.	
PSHE LO	To know what to do when a smoke alarm sounds. To know what to do if matches or a lighter are found. To know the correct number to report an emergency. To be able to identify two things in the home that can get hot.	To be able to identify two ways to prevent choking, etc. To recognise things that should not be worn around the neck when playing. To be able to list things which are safe/unsafe to put in your mouth.	To be able to state two rules for poisoning prevention.	To be able to state two ways to prevent falls when playing. To be able to identify two areas that are safe and unsafe to play in/near.	To understand the importance of telling a grown up if you find or see any weapons.	To understand why a cycle helmet is important when riding a bike. To know the correct procedure for crossing the road with a grown up.	To be able to identify a life jacket as an important item to wear when boating or taking part in an activity near water. To be able to state two water safety rules.
activity	Lesson 2 from Risk Watch Fire and Burn Prevention.	Lesson 3 from Risk Watch Preventing choking, suffocation and strangulation.	Lesson 4 from Risk Watch Poisoning Prevention.	Lesson 5 from Risk Watch Falls Prevention.	Lesson 6 from Risk Watch Weapons Injury Prevention.	Lesson 7 from Risk Watch Bike and Pedestrian Safety.	Lesson 8 from Risk Watch Water Safety.

Medium Term Planning

Theme: An Autumn Landscape with a view of Het Steen in the early morning   **Term: Autumn 2007**   **Year group: ONE**

Me and my world … Het Steen – the house in the painting

Focus	The house at Het Steen	Ollerton our homes	Life Education	Harvest	Once upon a painting
Subject	One 17-9-07	Two 24-9-07	Three 1-10-07	Four 8-10-07	Five 19-10-07
Literacy	A dark, dark tale		Poetry Nursery Rhymes	Labels and captions	Once upon a painting
Numeracy Unit 1	Block A	Block A	Block B	Block B	Block B
Science LO Materials	To know that materials have properties which can be recognised and described using appropriate vocabulary. To be able to ask questions and explore materials using appropriate senses. To know that there are many materials and these can be named and described. To understand that objects are made from materials and different everyday objects can be made from the same materials. To know that materials can be sorted in a variety of ways according to their properties. To be able to use the appropriate vocabulary to describe materials. To be able to make observations, communicate what happened, make predictions and draw conclusions.				
activity	Planned and taught by Sheila Lymbery using SOW.				
ICT LO Basic Skills	To be able to create an artefact with some help.			To be able to switch the computer off and on. To be able to use the keyboard with some help. To be able to print out work with some help.	
activity	Create own 'special person' badge.			Switch the PC on – type name – print out – switch off. Type and print labels and captions.	
RE LO Names, Christenings, Families	'Belonging' To know that they belong to different groups.	'Belonging' to a family. To know that they have a family name and a Christian name and that Christian children are baptised and given their Christian names.			
activity	Discuss being the 'Badger' team – how we can help each other when things start to go wrong.	Recording the members of their family – in pictures/names. Discussing what they know about baptism.			

DT **LO** Structures	To be able to use scissors accurately.		To be able to use a needle when sewing. To be able to use tools safely.	To be able to use cutting and joining skills to create an artefact.
activity	Cutting skills sheets-straight lines, zigzags and wavy lines.	Cutting skills- circles and triangles.	Sew material hearts/sheep. Baking jam tarts. Making heart shaped baskets.	Box models of houses – one box per group – cover with paper and turn into a house to represent the house in the painting. Link with history and science (materials). TASC activity.
History **LO** Old and new houses	To gain an understanding of the age of some houses.		To be able to use an artefact to gain a sense of time.	To begin to make comparisons between old and new houses. To be able to identify the key features of a home built a long time ago.
activity	Discuss 'Het Steen' – What clues tell us it is an old house? Literacy link to 'Dark, dark tale'.	Working with Ethel Swann.	Link back to first week and use painting to look for clues as to how we can tell whether something is old or modern.	Look at features of 'Het Steen' and find similarities and differences with their house. Visit Ollerton Hall to make similar comparisons. Draw their front door – compare with front door of 'Het Steen'.
Geography **LO** Our local area	To learn the layout of the school.	To be able to describe a route between 2 places in the local area.	To be able to use the painting as a focus for designing a simple route.	To be able to locate a country using an atlas/globe.
activity	Collecting and returning the register/messages at playtime.	Visit to the local library.	Map out a route through the painting.	Use an atlas or a globe to find the country featured in the painting.
Art **LO** Colour, line and shape	To be able to explore colour and texture.	To be able to mix a variety of shaded from a limited palette.	To be able to sketch from observation.	
activity	Sketching sheets 1 & 2. Begin to use pastels to create blocks of colour.	Colour mixing shades of grey to reflect the colours of the stone in the house in the painting.	Sketches of harvest fruits-pencil/ oil pastel.	

Subject / LO	Learning Objectives	Activity
Music LO Exploring skills, sounds and dynamics	To be able to sing in Unison. To use instruments to accompany a story.	To explore the different sounds they can make with their voices. To distinguish and perform different dynamics in a class performance.
activity	Establishing which songs they already know and looking at a new song – 'Only one can talk at a time'. During literacy create sound effects to accompany A Dark, Dark Tale.	Making different vocal sound effects at story time responding to a stop signal. Use 'We're going on a bear hunt' – children to echo the teacher's model. Can they distinguish and perform changes in dynamics and tempo. Use the story as the basis for our own story linked to the painting – 'We're going on a duck hunt' – can the children suggest sound effects and how we should make them. TASC activity.
PE GAMES LO	Multi-sports planned and taught by outside provider.	
activity		
PE GYM LO	To be able to bounce, hop, spring and jump using a variety of take offs and landings. To be able to observe, recognise and copy different body shapes. To be able to link together two or more actions with control and be able to repeat them. To be able to describe what they see using appropriate vocabulary.	
activity	PLANNED AND TAUGHT BY SUPPLY TEACHER USING VAL SABIN SOW.	
PE DANCE LO	To be able to listen to instructions. To be able to move in time to music. To be able to learn basic steps in a simple dance sequence.	
activity	Begin by listening to music and clapping in time, promenading, skipping, etc. Country dancing using skills of moving with a partner in different ways. As the term progresses begin to put many of the learned moves to create simple dances.	
DRAMA LO	To be able to respond to a stimulus.	To be a clear speaker. To be a good listener.
	To be able to create a still image. Link with SEAL – we are all part of the same team.	

activity			
'Freeze' game – remind chn about wobbling, eye contact and spacing.	**Black out hall.** Use 'Dark, Dark Tale' book as stimulus – read the beginning as far as the page with the statues. Recreate the scene with the children as statues. Model how to move through taking 1 or 2 chn. Encourage chn to change shape on my signal.	**Nursery Rhyme theme.** Using technique from previous session recreate different characters from Nursery Rhymes. Mime a character for others to guess who it is. Model this first.	Simple activities to encourage speaking and listening and observation. Repeat name over again whilst adult's hand moves up and down to indicate volume. Half the room stands still whilst others move around – when they come near someone they say, e.g. 'Hello, what's your name?' or 'Hello, where do you live?'

PSHE
LO
SEAL

NEW BEGINNINGS
To understand that they are all part of the class team.
To help make the class a safe and fair place and a good place to learn.
To understand that each of us contributes to the whole school community.

activity			
Introduce themselves to the group – my name is ... – how we listen and speak.	Drama link Understand how their actions have an impact on the whole group.	Sort out class target and golden time reward.	Class assembly – to gain a sense of everyone contributing.
			DT link How we behave when we are of the school premises – How well are we representing the school?

Finding out about horses

The special shire-horse

Focus	Divali		Light		Stars	Advent	Christmas	
Subject	**Six** 29-10-07	**Seven** 5-11-07	**Eight** 12-11-07	**Nine** 19-11-07	**Ten** 26-11-07	**Eleven** 3-12-07	**Twelve** 10-12-07	**Thirteen** 17-12-07
Literacy	Halloween spells, songs poems	Guy Fawkes Fireworks Bonfire night	Divali story	Owl Babies-retelling a story.	Instructions – star biscuits and lollipop stars. Why do stars come out at night?	Dick Whittington – preparation for Pantomime.	Christmas story Invitation to Christmas performance.	Christmas story
Numeracy Unit 1	Block D	Block D	Block D	Block E	Block E	Block E	Block C	Block C
Science LO Light	To know that light is essential for seeing things. To know that other senses can be used to find objects in the dark.	To be able to make comparisons between sources of light. To know that sources of light show up better at nighttime. To know there are many sources of light. To know that the sun is a powerful source of light for the earth. To know that shiny surfaces need a light source if they are to shine. To understand that shiny objects are not light sources.						
activity	Children to find objects in nursery shed. Round robin of activities	In small groups, find different sources of light around school. Read a story from a world religion linked to a festival of light. Make pictures linked to bonfire night. TASC activity. Sort shiny/non shiny materials. Explore mirrors and torches. BBC Science Clips – Light/Dark. ICT/RE link.						
ICT LO	To be able to load and use a paint package.			To be able to use a programmable toy.	To be able to use the keyboard and print out work with some help.	To be able to operate a listening centre.	To be able to use the internet to find information.	
activity	Creating a variety of pictures – Halloween, fireworks Rangoli patterns.			Using Bee-bots to follow a route linked to the story of Owl Babies.	Type a message for their Christmas card.	Listen to story of Dick Whittington.	Using www.communication4all.co.uk website to look at Advent Calendar and www.northpole for Christmas activities.	
RE LO	To understand that different faiths have different celebrations. To know that there is a faith known as Hinduism and that they celebrate Divali at this time. To know some of the traditions linked to Divali.			To understand that a church is a special place for Christians and the importance of showing respect for others and their special places.		To gain an understanding of the meaning of advent.	To understand the key elements of the Christmas story.	

activity	Discuss celebrations and note that some of them are linked to religions. Look at Divali story. Art and craft activities linked to Divali-Rangoli patterns, masks, diva lamps.			Church visit to St Paulinus. Prepare for church visit. Look at photographs of churches local and general. Discuss children's previous 'church' experiences. Understand the significance of different artefacts.		Making books about the Christmas story. TASC activity.
DT LO	To be able to create an artefact from malleable materials. To be able to use cutting and joining skills when creating an artefact. To be able to use kitchen tools with some help.			To be able to use basic joining techniques for 3D modelling using glues and masking tape. To know how to make structures more stable. To be able to use construction kits to aid modelling.	Making advent rings – start class advent calendar.	To be able to make simple hinges. To be able to use their own experience when developing ideas. To be able to clarify their ideas through discussion. To be able to make suggestions how to proceed. To be able to assemble, join and combine 2D and 3D materials into a model. To be able to use tools safely. To begin to evaluate the products they have made, commenting on the main features. TASC activity.
activity	Making Diva lamps (Clay). Halloween crafts – witches, hats, masks, cats, spider webs, etc. Make Halloween iced buns.			Make large whole class model of 'Het Steen'. TASC activity.		Children to make a simple stable and characters of the Nativity.
History LO	To begin to understand some of the customs linked to the festival of Halloween.	To understand key elements of the Gunpowder Plot.	To understand the key elements of the story of Rama and Sita.		To gain an understanding of the meaning of time passing – 'waiting' for an event to take place. RE link.	To understand the key elements of the Christmas story. To be able to use historical vocabulary.
activity	Discuss when Halloween originated and how it is celebrated nowadays. Make various artefacts, draw pumpkins, write spells, etc.	Drama link with teacher in role as Guy Fawkes. History DVD.	Drama link – tell the story of Rama and Sita and have the children act our different parts.		Discuss the meaning of advent as the advent ring is made.	Retelling the Christmas story through story writing, drama, art, music, etc. Use words such as first, then, next, after – to show 'time' passing.
Geography LO	To be able to recognise some physical features.		To be able to identify countries.			To be able to use a globe/world map to find countries.

activity	Use an altas or the globe to understand how sea/land are shown – notice the amount of sea compared with the amount of land.	Use globe or atlas to find the countries of India and Sri Lanka. (Also point out UK.)				RE link Use the globe/world map to show where the story of Jesus' birth took place. Also locate Egypt.
Art LO	To be able to sketch from observation. To be able to record patterns.		To record from first-hand observation and experience.			To begin to record from first-hand observation and explore ideas for a design. To represent their observations and ideas and design and make an interesting artefact.
activity	Observational sketches of pumpkins, spiders, Indian artefacts using pencil and oil pastels. Rangoli Patterns.		Sketch natural objects from around the school site – stones, twigs, leaves.			Various Christmas activities – cards, gift boxes, wreaths, etc. TASC activity.
Music LO	To be able to respond to a piece of music.			To be able to control pulse and rhythm.	To be able to control instruments.	To be able to sing in unison.
activity	Drama link – sing song 'Halloween's coming' and move as they different characters.	Listen to some music from India – how is it different from the music they like to listen to?	Listen to Handel's fireworks music – use a felt tip to 'draw' what they can hear in the music.	Drama link – Listen to Grieg's 'In the hall of the Mountain King'. What do they think the music is telling us? How would they move to this music? Clap in time to the music – noticing how it gets louder and faster towards the end of the piece.	Play the 'Quiet as a mouse' game with the children. See if the class can pass around a tambourine or jingles without making any sound.	Learn carols for the Christmas concert.
PE GAMES LO	Multi-sports planned and taught by outside provider.					
activity						
PE GYM LO	To be able to bounce, hop, spring and jump using a variety of take offs and landings. To be able to observe, recognise and copy different body shapes. To be able to link together two or more actions with control and be able to repeat them. To be able to describe what they see using appropriate vocabulary.					
activity	PLANNED AND TAUGHT BY SUPPLY TEACHER USING VAL SABIN SOW.					
PE DANCE LO	To be able to listen to and follow more than one instruction. To be able to move in time to music. To be able to learn basic steps in a simple dance sequence.					

activity	Continue to develop the country dancing skills of listening to music and clapping in time, promenading, skipping etc. Further develop country dancing using skills of moving with a partner in different ways. Continue to develop and improve dancing in circles of 8 or 4, moving forward and backwards in a line, making star shapes. Dancing up and down the lines, following round etc.			
DRAMA LO	To be able to create different characters.		To be able to work as part of a group.	To be able to work in role as a variety of characters.
activity	Sing the Halloween song and move around hall as the different characters.	Literacy link Recreate the Gunpowder plot – all children to be Guy Fawkes then in groups take on role of a 'plotter' and set up the barrels.	Literacy link Tell the story of Rama and Sita. The children then take on different roles and act as this character – Rama, Sita, Ravanna, Hanuman etc. TASC activity.	Literacy link Teacher to use Sarah, the oldest owl baby puppet to tell her story – living in a dark forest, mother leaving her and her brothers, how they felt, feelings when mother returned. Children to move in own way through the dark, scary forest.	Parachute activities. SEAL shark game.	Take on roles of different characters in the Nativity story building on skills learned at the beginning of this half term. Literacy/history link.
PSHE LO SEAL RISK-WATCH	To be able to work with others.	SEE LOs in Lesson Plan 2.	**GETTING ON AND FALLING OUT** 1. To be able to work well in a group. 2. To know what being a good friend means. 3. To be able to listen well when someone else is talking. 4. To know when they are starting to feel angry (how their body feels). 5. To know some ways to calm down when starting to feel angry. 6. To be able to make up with a friend after falling out. 7. To begin to use problem solving to sort out problems so both feel OK.	
activity	Country dancing link.	Risk Watch lesson – Fire and Burn Prevention	LO 1 & 2 Sharks game (P5) Hello and welcome game (P6)	LO 3 Revise speaking and listening rules and revamp list.	LO 4 & 5 Use story of where the wild things are.	LO 6 & 7 Class discussion on the best way to resolve issues.

Full TASC Wheel activities

Each term plan integrates a wide range of Learning Objectives, essential Basic Thinking Skills, Recording and Research skills, together with embedded thematic activities that allow the children to use the whole TASC Wheel Problem-solving Process. The children's learning experiences are linked across the curriculum and all science investigations lead to further cross-curricular activities. Importantly, the basic lesson plans are flexible since children are encouraged to direct their own learning.

All TASC activities are linked to hands-on experiential learning and the local environment. Expert mentors such as an artist, a forester and a farmer help the children to Gather and Organise information and develop appropriate skills. Secondary pupils act as story tellers and group leaders and parents are always invited to participate.

In assessing their work, the teachers, governors and parents report increased motivation and independence manifested by the children; and pupils demonstrate increasing confidence and fluency in using the TASC processes, transferring these processes and skills into all areas of the curriculum.

Science Ideas for full TASC Activities

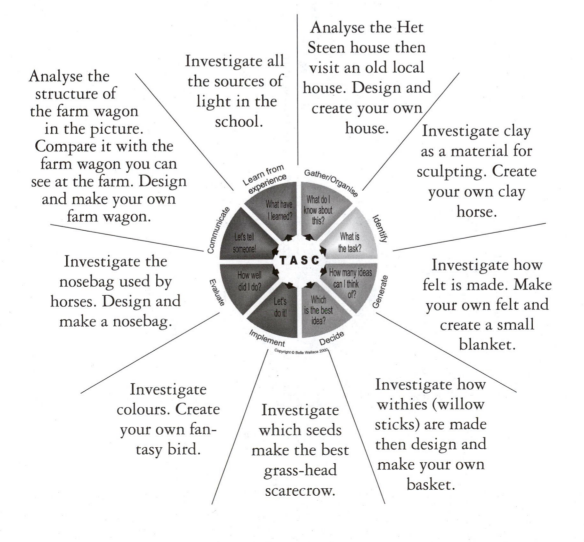

Analyse the Het Steen house then visit an old local house. Design and create your own house.

Investigate all the sources of light in the school.

Analyse the structure of the farm wagon in the picture. Compare it with the farm wagon you can see at the farm. Design and make your own farm wagon.

Investigate clay as a material for sculpting. Create your own clay horse.

Investigate the nosebag used by horses. Design and make a nosebag.

Investigate how felt is made. Make your own felt and create a small blanket.

Investigate colours. Create your own fantasy bird.

Investigate which seeds make the best grass-head scarecrow.

Investigate how withies (willow sticks) are made then design and make your own basket.

Creating our own birds

Investigating withies

This is Winston

This is Winston
he wiks hord
This is Winston
he is a shire horse.
This is Winston
he plods.
This is Winston
his bruther is at hom.
This is Winston
he has got a coler.
This is Winston
he lacs apuls.
This is Winston
he is 7.

a dentist hast to come to ceyn his teeth

ies 19 hand tall

He sleeps in a feyld

he black

he pulls logs

Winston worksi in a forst

he he plos

chends on

lws in a fom ferm

he is Make

his feprit fad is carrits

winston

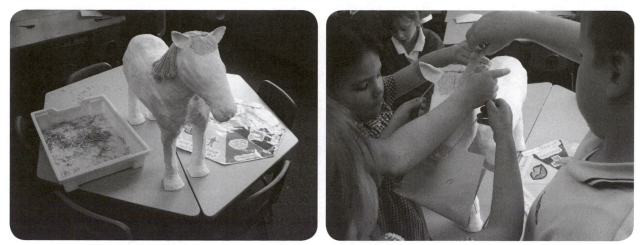

Investigating and making nosebags for our model horse

The house at Het Steen

Investigating which seeds make the best grass-head scarecrow

Analysing shapes in old houses

Working with the secondary students

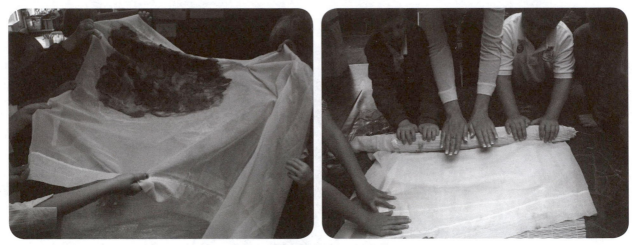

Making our own felt

FunTASCit through Science: Year 1: Exploring Materials
Example from Little Gonerby C/E Infants School, Lincolnshire

Headteacher: Elizabeth Wiggins

Class teachers and Teaching Assistants

Year 1: Marguerite Tibbett, Kirstie Cunningham and Jen Bayley.

The teachers of Year 1 plan together, integrating the learning objectives across the curriculum. This particular example highlights the focus on materials, using the story of '*Little Red Riding Hood*' as the stimulus.

Planning a TASC Topic on Materials

Week	Objectives	Main Teaching	Group Activities	Plenary	Resources / Links
1	Materials Gather information, Identify the task, Generate ideas, Decide on the best.	Ask questions about materials. Talk about materials and their properties. What do we know about bags? Who uses them? When do we use them and why? What do we do with them? Why are we investigating bags?	Look at a variety of different bags and discuss the properties. Group discussion. What is Little Red Riding Hood (LRH) taking to Grandma? Look again at bags and discuss which bags would be most suitable and why. Decide which is the best idea. (3 *'s and a wish).	What have we found out about properties?	Variety of bags. Camera. TASC Wheel, post it notes.
2	Materials Implement	Re-cap criteria for a strong bag with good handles for LRH. Remind children of TASC Wheel and our chosen idea.	Children to carry through plan and design their bag on paper first in pairs. Carry through plan of making bag. Monitor progress of design as children complete activity and change direction if necessary. Remind the children to keep in mind what they have to do next.	Talk about the progress made and discuss what comes next. How are they going to do it?	Camera, TASC Wheel, post-it notes, many different types of paper, glue, sellotape, scissors, stapler, design sheet, pencils.
3	Materials Evaluate	Consider the bags made by the children. Ensure children are in correct groups. Recap on the task.	Begin by discussing finished bag with original groups. Ask questions: What is good? What is not so good? How could you make it better next time? Give reasons for answer. Does it fulfil the task we set? Were the materials used suited to the task? Children to give their bag to another group for discussion. Same questions. Give opinion.	Spokesperson from each group to feed back to the rest of the class on their findings.	Camera, TASC Wheel, post-it notes, finished designs.
4	Materials Communicate, learn from experience	Children to participate in a school assembly to communicate their task. Children to discuss how they will do it differently next time.	Selection of children to show their bags and talk about what they had to do, what they used, how they made it, who it was for, what was good, what was not so good and what they would do differently next time.		Camera, TASC Wheel, post-it notes, finished bags.

Learning about materials

What names of materials do we know?
Tissue paper
Writing paper
Wood
Metal
Plastic
Feathers
Wool
Leather

What are materials used for?
Clothes
Shoes
Quilts
Curtains
Tables
Chairs

Walls
Pencils
Socks
Books
Bags

What are bags used for?
Why do we carry bags?
When do we use bags?
How can we carry bags?

Let's make a bag for Red Riding Hood to carry the things to Grandma's.

Gather/Organise

What do I know about this?

Identify

What is the task?

C

How many ideas can I think of?

Generate

Which is the best idea?

Decide

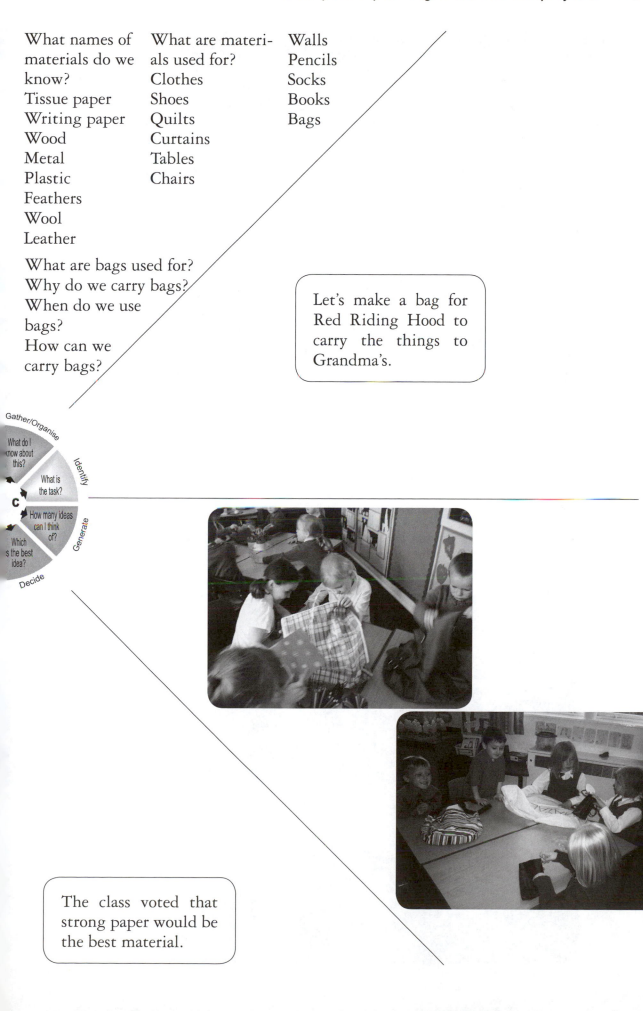

The class voted that strong paper would be the best material.

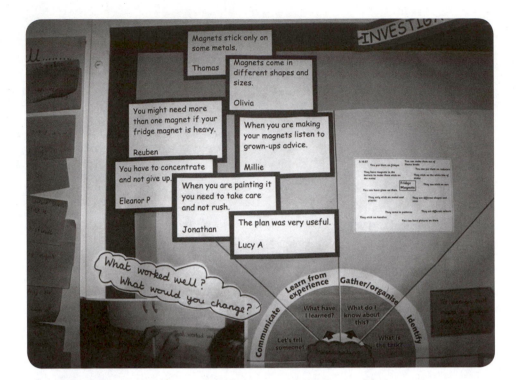

FunTASCit through Science: Foundation Phase: Exploring our Senses

Example from Little Gonerby C/E Infants School, Lincolnshire

Headteacher: Elizabeth Wiggins

Class teachers and teaching assistants

Reception Phase: Jane Anderson, Trish Odell, Helen Jackson, Catherine Goode, Hannah Longman, Charlotte Barber and Yvonne Whitty.

Planning across the Curriculum around the theme of Senses

TASC Senses Planning 1

Ic: R Classes 5/6 Weekly Plan – Term 2 Week 5 Planning for TASC Topic: The Senses

Science	Learning Obj:	Children to be able to identify their five senses	Success Criteria:	Children form a sentence about their news
		To understand how we use our senses to find out about the world around us		Children can identify characters and sequence events
		To investigate a question, using one of the five senses (touch)		
	Learning Obj:	To introduce children to share their news	Success Criteria:	Children form a sentence about their news
		To respond to a traditional tale		Children can identify characters and sequence events

Morning session 11.00–12.00

Mon

RB Complete guided writing/ Independent maths activity
YGO Guided Writing
Maths – Independent maths activity – ordering numbers to 6/10/15

Afternoon Session 1.00–2.20

Gather/Organise (What do I know about this?)
We need to choose a healthy snack for the Christmas party. To help us do this we need to think about taste
Brainstorm – What we already know about taste? (Whole class)
Do not lead the children – just accept volunteered answers.
Exploration of taste – children to explore a variety of tastes – salty crisp, lemon, icing, crackers, grapes, cheese. Generate vocabulary for texture and taste. (Groups)

Identify (What is the task?)
We're going to be scientists. What do scientists do? Find out and investigate and do experiments.
We've already been scientists when we found out about porridge – remind children of questions we asked and what we found out
What would we like to find out about taste? Can the children think of some questions? (Whole class)
We are going to investigate why we like certain tastes. Who can give an idea? Think of some of the words we used yesterday
Split into groups to record children's suggestions. Children draw favourite food, adult to annotate reason

Generate (How many ideas can I think of?)
Come back as a whole class, share some tastes
That's a lot of tastes! We can't try that many! Let's try and work out why we like certain tastes – Let's choose 3, and try and work out which is our favourite.
How can decide which of 3 tastes we like the most/the least, and in the middle? How are we going to do our experiment? Talk with a friend then share with a group. (Groups)

After play
Decide (Which is the best idea?)
2 methods of investigation
– Looking at food and ranking favourite, middle, least favourite (adult record)
– If we can see the food it might affect our choice – Use blindfolds and taste?

Tues
C6 num/lit
C5 topic

PE: Rawmarsh Lesson 8

Wed	**Implement** (Let's do it!) Split class into 2 groups – split colour groups Investigate different tastes – carrot, raisin, rice crispies. Children rank on a small recording sheet – indicate food by colour – orange-carrot, yellow-crispies, brown-raisin. (Groups) Blindfold group – 1:1 Adult to feed children, children to decide order of preference and record at end of test Normal group – 1:1 Children encouraged to discuss their preferences. Children to decide order of preference and record at end of test Adults annotate on labels for each child, expressing preferences Independent activities: Tough spot, selection of objects + magnifying glasses Microscope Natural objects in sand tray Dry! leaves in tough spot If dry – porridge oats out Feely objects in grey tray + feely box	**Big construction** Mobilo Big bricks Construct a car (+ PE shed) Duplo Castle Sponge Stickle bricks Number rods Wooden blocks
Thur	**Evaluate** (How well did we do?) Let's have a look at what we were tasting yesterday, some may have guessed already. What did we find out? We call what we found out our results Look at the results of the investigation Do results change for blindfold/non-blindfold? Let's give out the cards and find out what we thought. Share on carpet. Get children to stand/show hands/move in to groups to find out what was our favourite food, etc. Count **Communicate** (Let's tell someone!) (Whole class) I wonder if our results were the same as class 6/5? How are we going to show them what we have found? We can't all go and stand in their class. What else could we do? Record numbers/gummed coloured paper/ faces on food pictures/ Use 2 simple to make a graph	Tough spot, selection of objects + magnifying glasses Microscope Natural objects in sand tray Bark in tough spot with the minibeasts If dry – porridge oats out Feely objects in grey tray + feely box Sand tray Leaf rubbings Food sort – like dislike Senses books Shakers (See Jane)
Fri	**Learn from experience** (What have we learned?) What new things have we learned about taste? Adding to brainstorm in a different colour. (Whole class) What do we feel about different tastes? What have we learned about doing an experiment?	Gardening afternoon

Make badges for children: Class 6 scientist + clip art picture.
Get clipboards out.
Camera – batteries charged, memory stick empty!

TASC Senses Planning 2		
Theme/ Topic: Our Senses	**Early Learning Goals:** KUW 4 Investigate places, objects, materials and living things by using all of their senses as appropriate. Identifies some features and talks about those features they like/dislike. KUW 5 Ask questions about why things happen and how things work. Look closely at similarities, differences, patterns and change.	
Learning objectives	**Activities**	**Vocabulary**
Children should: Be able to identify their five senses. To understand how we use our senses to find out about the world around us. To investigate a question, using one of the five senses (touch)	**Sight:** Explore how we use our eyes to see Looking through microscope for whiteboard, magnifying glasses Looking through filters, goggles, sunglasses What would I miss if I were blind – working with a partner – one blindfolded – put things in places/walk around and step over **Touch:** Feely box – which part of our hand are we using to touch? Walk around school to find – smooth, rough, soft, hard. Sorting by texture (encourage children to close their eyes when handling the materials) – encourage language smooth, rough, hard, soft, bumpy, slippery, fluffy, dry, etc. **Hearing:** Explore hearing. How do we hear? What can we hear? Identifying sounds - Sound lotto Guess the instrument Copy the rhythm Environmental sounds **Smell:** Brainstorm – How does smell help us? (Helps us enjoy our food, keeps us safe, e.g. warns us when food is bad or if things are burning). We use our nose to smell so it's hard to smell if we have a cold Guess the smell – lemon/vinegar/lavender/nutmeg, etc. Draw out descriptive language **Taste:** Explore how we use our tongue to taste. Different areas of our tongue pick up different tastes – bitter/ sweet/salty/sour. Taste test. Focus on descriptive language, e.g. sweet/ salty/spicy/sour, etc.	Names of senses Names of parts of body associated with each sense Descriptive language for each sense, especially touch and taste
		Resources
		Magnifying glasses Filters Goggles Sunglasses Blindfolds Feely Box Variety of objects to explore by touch (sandpaper, cones, shells sponge wool, etc.) Sound lotto Instruments Found objects Cups/cotton wool, scent sources (e.g. lemon, nutmeg, ginger, vinegar, lavender) Foods to taste (Christmas foods, e.g. mince, dates, marzipan) (CHECK FOOD ALLEGIES) Books about the senses
	Key Questions	**Next Steps**
	How does it look/feel/sound/smell/taste..? What part of our body do we use to help us it look/ feel/sound/smell/taste ..? What do we know already? What do we want to find out? How can we find out? What have we learned?	

The Foundation Phase staff of Little Gonerby Infants School plan as a team, integrating the six areas of learning:

☐   Personal, social and emotional development

☐   Communication, language and literacy

☐   Mathematical development

☐   Knowledge and understanding of the world

☐   Physical development

☐   Creative development.

The children's activities are integrated across the curriculum, and as often as is possible, the children direct their own learning.

Gather and Organise: Discussing what we know about food and why we like some foods more than others

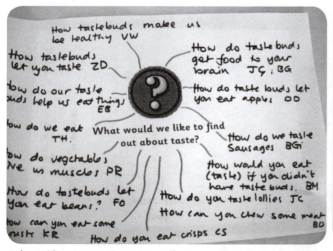

Identify: Learning to ask questions and identifying what we would like to find out

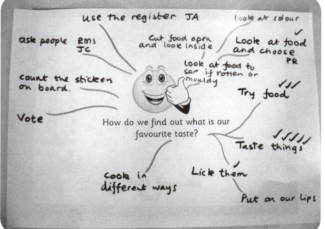

Generate: Thinking about how we could find out the answers to our questions

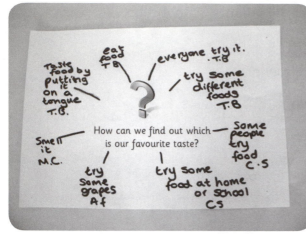

Decide: Trying to decide how to conduct our experiments

Implement: Can we taste if we cannot see?

Carefully observing my tongue   Implement: How much can my hands tell me?

Implement: Which is my favourite food?

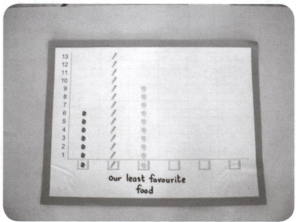

Communicate: Learning to record visually

Communicate: Learning to record on a block graph

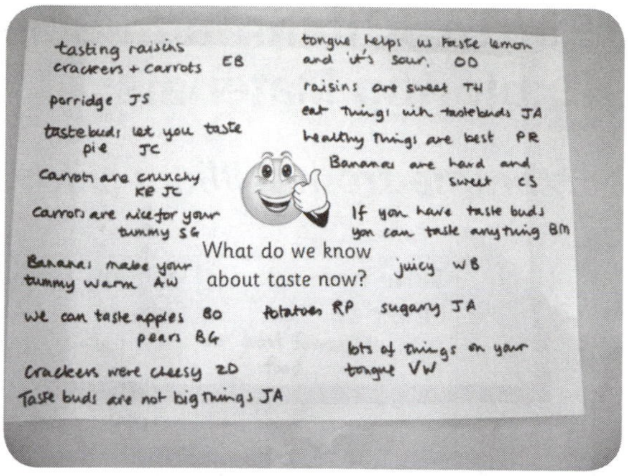
tasting raisins crackers + carrots EB
porridge JS
taste buds let you taste pie JC
Carrots are crunchy KB JC
Carrots are nice for your tummy SG
Bananas make your tummy warm AW
we can taste apples BO pears BG
Crackers were cheesy ZD
Taste buds are not big things JA
tongue helps us taste lemon and it's sour. OD
raisins are sweet TH
eat things with tastebuds JA
healthy things are best PR
Bananas are hard and sweet CS
If you have taste buds you can taste anything BM
What do we know about taste now?
juicy WB
potatoes RP
sugary JA
lots of things on your tongue VW

Learn from Experience: What do we know now?

My taste investigation
1st
2nd
3rd
Name: Eleanor
w/c 26.11.07

FunTASCit through Science: Year 2: Exploring Materials

Example from William Hildyard C/E Primary School

	Time needed: One day	William Hildyard C/E Primary School Teacher: Sally-Ann Lucas Curriculum Area: Knowledge and understanding Year	Cross-curricular/ PSHE links Group development Measuring Listening and speaking Practical skills Drawing plans
POS	**Learning Objectives:** Ask questions and decide how to answer them Use first hand experience to answer them Recognise when a 'test' is unfair Find out about the properties of materials		**Vocabulary** fair test, unfair test compare stronger, weaker trialling, adapting predicting because statement
	Introduction: Gather and Organise: What do I already know about this? Listen to '3 Little pigs' story, Discuss properties of straw, sticks and bricks for building houses		
	Activity: Identify: What is the task? Can we build a strong house with the materials we have in the classroom? (straw, lego blocks, cereal cartons, small sticks, tinfoil, various fabrics, polystyrene, wool, plus materials in the classroom identified by the children) A strong fan and stopwatch Generate: How many ideas can I think of? Group discussion of possible ideas for a house Discussion of what would be a 'fair test' Decide: Which is the best idea? Each group to decide on their best idea and to sketch it Implement: Let's do it! Making houses, testing their strength, making changes and re-testing Communicate: Let's tell someone! Make a display and tell Year 1 about the TASC Process Plenary Evaluate: How well did I do? Learn from experience What have we learned about building? What have we learned about materials? Have we worked well together? What have we learned about asking questions? What are we pleased with? What would we do better next time?		**Differentiation** Mixed ability groups Outcome **Support** Support with TA **Resources** TASC Wheel on whiteboard straw, lego blocks, cereal cartons, small sticks, tinfoil, various fabrics, polystyrene, wool
	Observations The whole class needs more practice in asking questions Some children didn't understand 'compare' The children were on task the whole day. This included the children who usually find it difficult to concentrate We needed to discuss the concept of stable base'		

FunTASCit through Science: Years 1 and 2: Magnets

Example from Gonerby Hill Foot CE Primary School

PLANNING A TASC PROJECT		
Gonerby Hill Foot C/E Primary Schoo	**Curriculum Area** Science D.T.	Cross-curricular/PSHE links Art Speaking and Listening
Year Groups 1 and 2	**Learning Objective** To make a fridge magnet	
Gather and organise: Look at examples of fridge magnets. Investigate magnets and materials **Identify:** Task – to create a fridge magnet	**Vocabulary** Fridge magnet, attract, repel, magnetic metal, force, properties, materials	
Generate: Discuss magnets and generate four designs to choose from **Decide:** Select one design to make **Implement:** Practise with play dough before using model magic	**Extension:** ICT to be used for research and planning. Other modeling materials available	
Evalute: Test magnet. Evaluate effectiveness and appearance of finished product **Communicate:** Individual showing to class and sharing of experiences. Photos display for rest of school	**Support** Extra adult support	
Learn from experience: What have I learned? Discussion of skills learnt and improvements that could be made next time	**Resources** Play dough Model magic Small magnets Paint, PVA glue Brushes Design sheet	
Notes/Implications for future planning Use of transferable skills in other areas of the curriculum	**Key Assessment** Children's responses to TASC project	

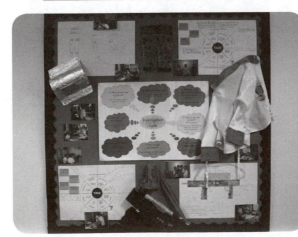 

Testing my fridge magnet.

What worked well? What would you change?

We had lots of ideas!

Finding out how magnets work.

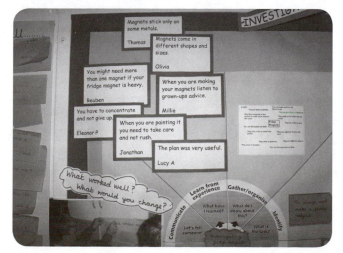

Magnets stick only on some metals.

Thomas

Magnets come in different shapes and sizes.

Olivia

You might need more than one magnet if your fridge magnet is heavy.

Reuben

When you are making your magnets listen to grown-ups advice.

Millie

You have to concentrate and not give up.

Eleanor P

When you are painting it you need to take care and not rush.

Jonathan

The plan was very useful.

Lucy A

What worked well? What would you change?

FunTASCit through Science: Foundation Phase: Autumn

Example from Little Gonerby CE Primary School

PLANNING A TASC PROJECT		
Gonerby Hill Foot C/E Primary Schoo	**Curriculum Area** Knowledge and Understanding of the World	Cross-curricular/PSHE links Caring for the environment
Year Group Foundation Stage	Learning Objective To recall what the children know about autumn and extend their knowledge for the purpose of making a display	
Gather and organise: Whiteboard – What do we know? Brainstorm **Identify:** What are we going to find out about autumn?	**Vocabulary** Autumn Season Conker Leaf Hibernation	
Generate: How are we going to find out about autumn? Brainstorm **Decide:** We need to think about the best way to find out information and vote on an appropriate method	**Extensioin** Classification of finds Research on leaves, etc.	
Implement: Autumn Walk – take photos and collect things **Evaluate:** Whiteboard – What do we know now?	**Support** LSA and teaching support	
Communicate: Display about autumn **Learn from experience: What have I learned?** Post-its with a range of reflections on display	**Resources** Tracing paper Conkers Leaves Paint Paper	
Notes/Implications for future planning Visual display particularly effective in communicating methods and outcomes	**Key Assessment** FS profile – Knowledge and Understanding of the World	

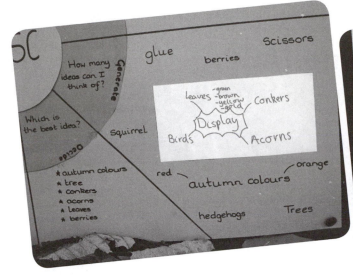
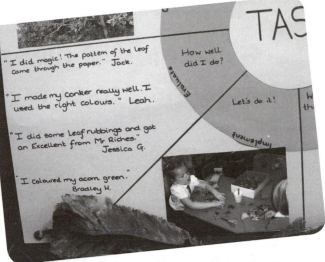

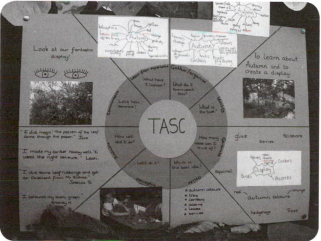
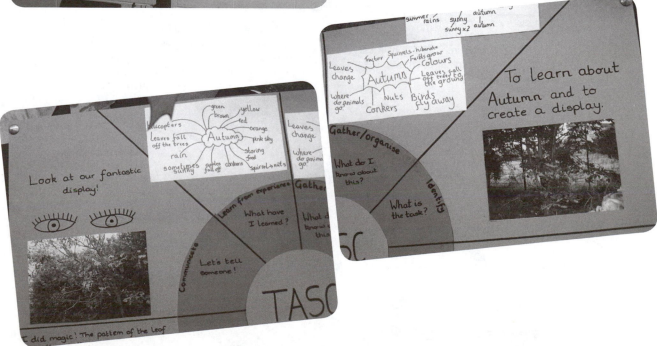

Chapter 5

Examples of planning TASC science projects: Key Stage 2

FunTASCit through Science: Year 3: Investigating woodlice

Example from Ollerton Primary School

Why do woodlice live in the places we found them?

Are there any changes we could make to our investigations to make it better? Are there any new questions to investigate?
Answer questions from audience. Decide if results are conclusive. Does anything remain to be tested?

What do we know about woodlice? Where did we find them?
In groups with large paper on floor, write/draw/discuss experience at Perlethorpe and feedback. What are the features of those places? How would you describe them?

How can we show what we found to other people?
Prepare to show audience results – draw, talk, video, model, demonstrate, etc.

Why do the woodlice like living where we found them?
In groups with large paper on floor, write/draw/discuss ideas and feedback. Do we know which of our ideas is right?

What do our results tell us about what woodlice like?
Did our investigation work?
Discuss results with partner.

How can we find out which of our ideas is right?
In pairs, draw/label/model/ discuss and develop ways to investigate theories. Will the test answer the question?

Lets try out our test.
Pairs to conduct their investigation, collecting resources and constructing equipment. Think about how to record results.

Which of our ideas will work the best? Can we get everything we need?
Decide which idea will work the best, thinking about availability of resources and will results answer question. How will we observe the results?

Why do you live in the places where we found you?

FunTASCit through Science: Year 5: Cleaning dirty water

Example from Ollerton Primary School

TASC Week Planning: Ollerton Primary School – Year 5: Cleaning dirty water

Learning objective	Learning opportunity	Differentiation	Key vocabulary
Wednesday: To plan and carry out an experiment to test which material is the most effective at cleaning dirty water. **Thursday:** To carry out an experiment and record findings. **Friday:** To evaluate their own work.	**Gather/organise:** Using the 'gather/organise' section of the TASC Wheel – ask children to consider everything that might affect how affective a material is at cleaning water. **Identify:** Fill in 'identify' section with the task given – how can we clean this dirty water? **Generate:** Children to discuss: Which material is most effective at filtering dirty water? What resources will we need? How could we do the experiment? **Decide:** Discuss ideas from the 'generate' stage in groups. Decide on the best/most practical ideas. Decide on plan of action. **Implement:** In small groups children to carry out the experiment and record findings, and decide how they are going to present their findings. **Evaluate/communicate/reflect:** Share findings and agree on a conclusion. Fill in questionnaire: What have you found out? What have you enjoyed? What could you have improved on? Circle time to discuss answers.	TA support outcome resources teacher support	gather organise identify generate evaluate fair test conclusion prediction material effective

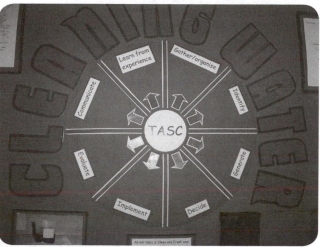

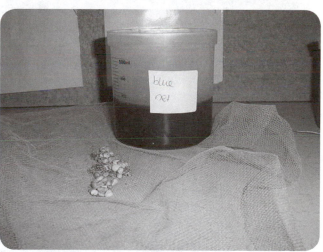

FunTASCit through Science: Year 4/5: Solids, liquids, gases

Example from Ropley Primary School

Ropley CE Primary School

Medium Term Curriculum Planning

Science years 4/5 Spring 2008 Solids, liquids and gases

Key Ideas	Vocabulary		Research Study Outcome	TASC
Solids, liquids and gases (QCA 4D + 5C + 5D) • Solids, liquids and gases are defined by certain properties • Gases have mass (and weight on Earth) • Materials of different size can be separated by filtering and sieving • Evaporation and condensation are reversible changes • Melting and freezing/solidification are reversible changes • The water on Earth goes through a cycle involving all three states	3/4 property solid liquid gas reversible irreversible dissolve solution solute solvent soluble insoluble sediment suspension melt freeze condensation evaporation sieve filter separate mixture pure	5/6 air boiling temperature bubbles carbon dioxide change change of state condense conditions dissolve evaporate filter hazard heat mixture oxygen solidify state steam water cycle	More opportunities to use and apply skills, knowledge and understanding in new contexts To collaborate as a group to plan approaches to problem solving To decide the best means of presenting group work from a variety of known strategies To know and develop the use of different roles within a group Subject Leader Action Plan Use a range of ways of recording results • Decide what observations/measurements are needed • Decide how many measurements are needed • Select appropriate equipment from a range • Present results clearly using graphs and tables • Decide on an appropriate method of recording • Put results in stick graphs or simple line graphs.	Use the TASC Wheel to help improve the children's investigative skills. **Gather/organise:** What do I know that I can use in a new context? **Identify:** What is the task? What variables/factors need to be kept the same, changed, measured? **Generate:** How many ways can I think of going about this investigation/solving this problem? **Decide:** What will I do? Implement: Carry out plan of investigation/task and collect data **Evaluate:** Use results to draw conclusions. Was it a fair test? Is the data accurate? Is there anything I would change if I repeated the investigation? Is there anything else I would like to do to learn more? **Communicate:** Present results and findings **Learn from experience:** • Science? • team work? • individual thinking skills?

Skills – identify factors involved, record results in a range of ways, use results to draw conclusions

Focus	Learning Objectives	Suggested Activities	Assessment and Key Questions
9 Jan	• The water on Earth goes through a cycle involving all three states • Evaporation and condensation are reversible changes • Melting and freezing/solidification are reversible changes	What happens to a glacier? TASC question, use Wheel!! Give children a block of ice. Observe melting (in water, on rock, on soil?) What happens to water? Observe	How do children record results? Record results Explain water cycle Generate ideas for a range of ideas using Sc K & U Record results Explain filtering and sieving Diagram of balloons with explanation
15 Jan	Communicate and learn from experience	Follow-up from last week Discuss ways of recording results Draw conclusions	
23 Jan (Calshot)	Topic related task Evaporation – investigate factors: wind, temperature, surface area	Observe model of water cycle	
29 Jan 5 Feb 12 Feb Electricity next – short unit, so may extend this work!	• Materials of different size can be separated by filtering and sieving • Gases have mass (and weight on Earth) • Solids, liquids and gases are defined by certain properties	Observe melting and solidification Observe evaporation and condensation Use model to explain water cycle Year 5s finish writing diary Year 4s create a poster explaining the water cycle Input from Science clips Design a gravel sorting machine to grade for size Design a sewage treatment plant to extract solids from water Make above and record results Prepare presentation for buyers What have I learnt? Individual explanation of filtering and sieving Class demonstration of weight of gas (weigh balloon with and without air!) Define properties.	

FunTASCit through Science: Year 5/6: Forces

Example from Ropley Primary School

Ropley CE Primary School

Medium Term Curriculum Planning

Science Yr 5/6 Autumn 2007 Forces in Action (linked 6E)

Key Ideas	Basic Skills	Advanced Skills	Research Study Outcome	TASC
Review 3E, 4E, 4F • Weight is a force. • Several forces can act on one object. • Gravitational attraction causes objects to have weight. • Forces acting on an object can change direction, speed up or slow down movement. • There are forces between magnets. • A spring exerts a force when stretched or compressed. • Elasticity is a force. • Friction is a force which occurs when two surfaces rub together.	Push Pull Stationary Moving Direction Travel Surface Grip Tread Speed Faster Slower Stretch Spring	Newton Friction Magnetism Attraction Repulsion Elasticity Compress Extend Air resistance Water resistance Surface area Lubrication Gravity Weight Up-thrust Force-meter	More opportunities to use and apply skills, knowledge and understanding in new contexts To collaborate as a group to plan approaches to problem solving To decide the best means of presenting group work from a variety of known strategies To know and develop the use of different roles within a group	Use the TASC Wheel to help improve the children's investigative skills. **Gather/Organise:** What do I know that I can use in new context? **Identify:** What is the task? What variables/factors need to be kept the same, changed, measured? **Generate:** How many ways can I think of going about this investigation/ solving this problem? **Decide:** What will I do? **Implement:** Carry out investigation/task and collect data. **Evaluate:** Use results to draw conclusions. Was it a fair test? Is the data accurate? Is there anything I would change if I repeated the investigation? Is there anything else I would like to do to learn more? **Communicate:** Present results and findings. **Learn from experience:** • science • team work • individual thinking skills

Recording Skills – use arrows to represent the size and direction of forces – record observations and measurements accurately and clearly – look for patterns.

Focus	Learning Objectives	Suggested Activities	Assessment and Key Questions
31 Oct Introduction 7 Nov 14 Nov Upthrust 21 Nov Elasticity 28 Nov (assembly visitor) Air resistance 5 Dec (Christmas lunch)	Identify weight as a force and the newton (N) as the unit in which it is measured: • Gravitational attraction causes objects to have weight. • A spring exerts a force when stretched or compressed. • Weight is a force. • Several forces can act on one object. • Friction is a force which occurs when two surfaces rub together. • Several forces can act on one object. • Elasticity is a force. Forces acting on an object can change direction, speed up or slow down movement. • Science is important because the more we understand about something the more we can do with it.	**Gather/Organise** Brainstorm forces. Make concept map. **Generate ideas** Why do people seem weightless in space? Watch Sc dvd clips. Discuss gravity and draw diagram. **Decide and Implement** Use force meter. Weigh objects in air and water. Diagram using arrows to show forces. Record results using own format. **Communicate and Reflect on Learning** Boat design – upthrust/gravity. Investigate upthrust. Diagram using arrows to show forces. Results table. Make a force meter using elastic bands. Diagram using arrows to show forces. Results table. Repeat measurements. Line graph. Discussion. Parachute or spinner investigation. Diagram using arrows to show forces. Results table. Repeat measurements. Communicate: advertisement for a parachute. Make a toy using knowledge and understanding of the science of forces.	Record observations of the effects of gravity • Explain why people seem weightless in space and how gravity keeps them on Earth. • Describe the forces acting on a stationary object, produce annotated drawings showing the direction in which forces are acting. • Record force meter readings for objects suspended in air and in water and identify that the reading in water is less than that in air. • Explain why an object appears to weigh less when it is immersed in water than when it is in air, e.g., the upward push of the water cancels out some of the weight or 'pull down from gravity'. • Make a series of measurements of the length of the elastic band with forces applied. • Represent data in a line graph. • Identify a trend in the graph, e.g., the heavier the weight, the more it stretches and use patterns to make predictions. • Recognise that measurements of the same quantity can vary. • Identify some reasons for variation, e.g., sometimes the pointer isn't steady. • State that they have more confidence in results when repeated measurements are close together. ALL MUST Identify weight as a force; Recognise that more than one force can act on an object; measure forces using a force-meter and present measurements in tables. MOST WILL Identify that weight is a force and is measured in newtons; Describe some situations in which there is more than one force acting on an object; Draw diagrams to illustrate forces acting on an object; Use a force-meter accurately to measure forces; Present measurements in simple line graphs, identify patterns in these and evaluate explanations. SOME WILL EXTEND TO Describe and explain the motion of some familiar objects in terms of several forces acting on them.

FunTASCit through Science: Year 5/6: Light and Micro-organisms

Example from Ropley Primary School

Ropley CE Primary School

Medium Term Curriculum Planning

Science Yr 5/6 Spring 2008 Light (short unit) Micro-organisms (short unit)

Key Ideas	Basic Skills	Advanced Skills	Research Study Outcome	TASC
Shadows are formed when light is blocked. Light travels in a straight line. We see because light enters out eyes. Surfaces can absorb or reflect light. When a beam of light is reflected from a surface, its direction changes. Micro-organisms feed, grow and reproduce. There are beneficial and harmful micro-organisms. Nutrition cycles depend on the action of micro-organisms.	light light beam mirror opaque transparent translucent light source shadow ray reflection	fertiliser germ growth health life cycle petal microbe nutrients nutrition reproduction/ reproduce teeth virus plaque	More opportunities to use and apply skills, knowledge and understanding in new contexts. To collaborate as a group to plan approaches to problem solving. To decide the best means of presenting group work from a variety of known strategies. To know and develop the use of different roles within a group. **Subject Leader Action Plan** Use a range of ways of recording results: <ul><li>Decide what observations/ measurements they need to make.</li><li>Decide how many measurements they need to make.</li><li>Select appropriate equipment from a range.</li><li>Present results clearly using graphs and tables.</li><li>Decide on an appropriate method of recording.</li><li>Put results in stick graphs or simple line graphs.</li></ul>	Use the TASC Wheel to help improve the children's investigative skills. **Gather/Organise:** What do I know that I can use in a new context? **Identify:** What is the task? What variables/factors need to be kept the same, changed, measured? **Generate:** How many ways can I think of going about this investigation/ solving this problem? **Decide:** What will I do? **Implement:** Carry out investigation/task and collect data. **Evaluate:** Use results to draw conclusions. Was it a fair test? Is the data accurate? Is there anything I would change if I repeated the investigation? Is there anything else I would like to do to learn more? **Communicate:** Present results and findings. **Learn from experience:** <ul><li>science</li><li>team work</li><li>individual thinking skills</li></ul>

Skills: repeat measurements for reliability.

Focus	Learning Objectives	Suggested Activities	Assessment and Key Questions
27 Feb Light sources Shiny and dull surfaces.	We see light sources because light from them enters our eyes. Surfaces can absorb or reflect light. Shiny surfaces can be used as mirrors.	Experiment with torch beams and a variety of shiny and dull surfaces. Light travels in a straight line. We see because light enters our eyes. **TASC**	Describe shiny surfaces as mirrors; highly polished surfaces as good reflectors. Dull surfaces cannot be used as mirrors.
5 Mar Shadows	Identify factors which might affect the size and position of the shadow of an object. Investigate how changing one factor causes a shadow to change. To consider trends in results and decide whether there are results which do not fit the pattern. To check measurements by repeating them.	Investigate shadow sizes. **TASC**	Show in drawings that light travels in a straight line and explain factors that can affect the size of the shadow.
12 Mar Reflected light 19 March SCAT hat day (link Easter?)	When a beam of light is reflected from a surface, its direction changes. Light from an object can be reflected by a mirror, the reflected light enters our eyes and we see the object.	Shine a beam of light at a mirror and look at angle of reflection. Safety: do not shine light into eyes. Use sc dvd clips and study guides for beneficial and harmful micro-organisms. Grow yeast, observe gas bubbles produced, and increased amount of yeast (filtering).	Explain in a diagram how a mirror can change the direction of a light beam, representing the direction in which the light beam travels by an arrow. Describe life cycle of yeast.
26 March Micro-organisms 2 April	Micro-organisms feed, grow and reproduce. There are beneficial and harmful micro-organisms. Nutrition cycles depend on the action of micro-organisms.	Look at recycling and composting in the school – what would happen if there were no micro-organisms. Why doesn't plastic and metal decompose in the same way? **TASC**	Explain how nutrition cycles depend on the action of micro-organisms.

Chapter 6

Further ideas for developing TASC projects

Any curriculum topic can be planned to incorporate TASC Problem-solving activities. Some TASC activities can be planned using the whole TASC Wheel; while other activities may possibly use only segments of the TASC Wheel. The following full TASC projects have all been carried out in schools across the country.

Celebrating sunhats and sunglasses

Creating a minibeast

Create a sense garden

Create moving toys

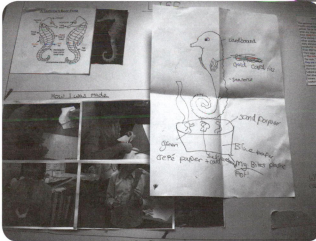

Design a sea creature

Explore the water cycle

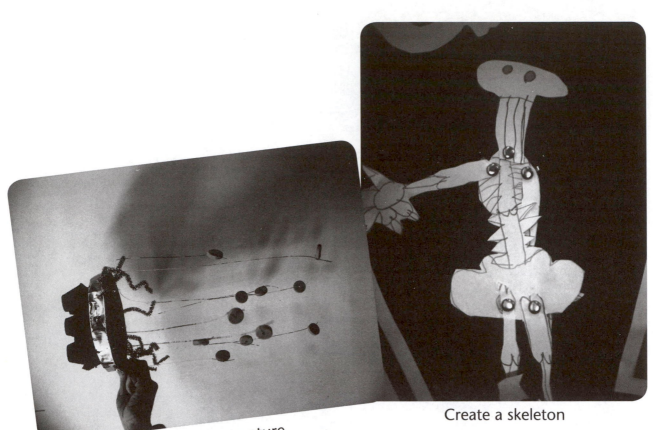

Design a sea creature

Create a skeleton

Musical Instruments

Grow different kinds of seeds

Design and trial musical instruments

Grow hair on a monster

Investigate bats

Investigate biscuits

Investigate bones

Investigate energy

Create a pond scoop

Design and trial kites

Conclusion

The greatest gifts we can give to any learner are the gifts of self-esteem, self-reliance and the confidence to solve problems in the belief that learning for life is a process of continual re-thinks until a suitable answer or solution is found. I am sure that teachers who witness the growth of learners' problem-solving skills derive a deep sense of professional and personal fulfilment from the living evidence of seeing learners' developing greater competence and eventual mastery of their thinking and problem-solving processes. I am equally sure that teachers who work within the TASC Problem-solving Framework feel a great sense of liberation in that they have a flexible and sound frame-work within which to plan for greater flexibility across the curriculum: to give the children their voice, to negotiate learning pathways and to differenti-ate learning activities across the full range of multiple abilities. The essence of the TASC Framework is the celebration of *all* pupils' gifts and talents. And I believe that the primary role of teachers is to provide opportunities for *all* pupils to discover their gifts ... whether these gifts are like soft candle flames or brilliant torches of light. All children are more efficient learners when they have opportunities to celebrate their strengths; and when they can confidently discuss their weaknesses knowing that everyone has weaknesses, but there is support and care at hand to strengthen them. The TASC Framework is abso-lutely in line with the government document *Every Child Matters* (DFES 2004), and encourages inclusivity alongside differentiation.

The TASC Framework was conceived and developed throughout the 1980s and early 1990s with many groups of disadvantaged learners in what was then the Apartheid 'homeland' of KwaZulu Natal. However, when I returned to the UK in the latter part of 1998, I found disadvantage on a massive scale.

Certainly, in the UK, children are entitled to free education and are largely well-fed and clothed; but many learners are deprived of rich early years' experiential learning and opportunities for rich language development that form the foundation for further learning. In addition, so many families are fragmented, incomes are often inappropriately spent and the rise of incidents of violence and anti-social behaviour are ever on the increase.

Much has been written about the challenges of today's classrooms, and I believe that one of the most important means of beginning to meet these challenges is to work with children and young people within the paradigm of problem-solving and thinking skills. Learners need to be closely involved in their education – to be partners in what they are learning and why – to have a voice in decision-making about how they best learn and about what interests them.

All the examples of working within the TASC Framework – so willingly shared by the schools cited in this book, report that learners have acquired greater motivation, enjoyment and resilience. The teachers say that they have a greater enjoyment in teaching more creatively and flexibly. Teachers also claim that they have seen many children in a new light and have been surprised at the commitment brought to the problem-solving tasks the children have undertaken. Often, the teacher has been the facilitator rather than the dispenser of inert knowledge and the learners have thrived in the process of Thinking Actively in a Social Context.

The TASC Framework is a cross-curricular framework and the science projects throughout the book have all had appropriate cross-curricular extensions. I hope that we have conveyed the practical know-how of working in the TASC way!

I acknowledge the great work of Diana Cave and Andrew Berry, together with the schools that have made such worthwhile contributions. The book is dedicated to teachers who are working so hard to overcome the challenges that face us; and to the children who are tomorrow's world.

Belle

Reference

Department for Education and Skills (2004) *Every Child Matters: Change for Children in Schools.* Nottingham, DFES.

Appendix 1

TASC Publications:

Wallace B (2002) Teaching Thinking Skills Across the Early Years
London: David Fulton Publishers (A NACE-Fulton Pub) ISBN 1 85346 842 8

Wallace B (2001) Teaching Thinking Skills Across the Primary Curriculum
London: David Fulton Publishers (A NACE-Fulton Pub) ISBN 1 85346 766 9

Wallace B (2002) Teaching Thinking Skills Across the Middle Years
London: David Fulton Publishers (A NACE-Fulton Pub) ISBN 1 85346 767 7

Wallace B (2003) Using History to Develop Thinking Skills at Key Stage 2
London: David Fulton Publishers (A NACE-Fulton Pub) ISBN 1 85346 928 9

Wallace B and Maker J, et al. (2004) Thinking Skills and Problem-Solving:
An Inclusive Approach
London: David Fulton Publishers (A NACE-Fulton Pub) ISBN 1 84312 107 7

TASC Classroom Products

Large A0 size laminated classroom TASC Posters.

TASC Wheel Poster (A2) and 15 Wipe-Clean TASC Boards for pupils.

TASC DVD in which children explain how they have used TASC, and a CDRom with examples of TASC lesson plans.

TASC C/A poster with 15 file copies that show how TASC dovetails with the Elements of the NACE Challenge Award.

Specific TASC Training is also available for schools working towards:

☐ a whole school policy of Inclusion and classroom Differentiation

☐ Personalised Learning

☐ Specific subject and cross-curricula TASC planning

☐ Raising Standards

These publications, products and services are all available from:

TASC International

28 St Stephen's Hill. Canterbury, Kent CT2 7AX, UK

Appendix 2

The full TASC problem-Solving Process

Appendix 3

The TASC Framework

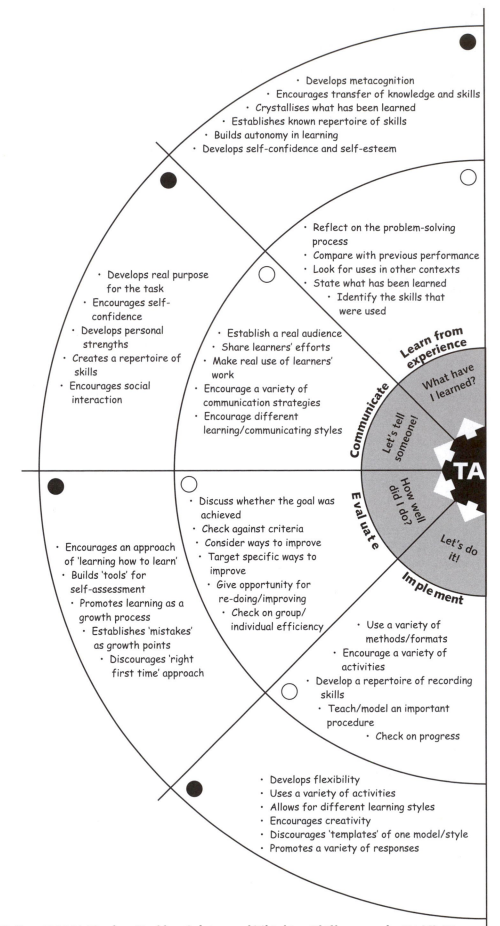

· Develops metacognition
· Encourages transfer of knowledge and skills
· Crystallises what has been learned
· Establishes known repertoire of skills
· Builds autonomy in learning
· Develops self-confidence and self-esteem

· Develops real purpose
  for the task
· Encourages self-
  confidence
· Develops personal
  strengths
· Creates a repertoire of
  skills
· Encourages social
  interaction

· Reflect on the problem-solving
  process
· Compare with previous performance
· Look for uses in other contexts
· State what has been learned
· Identify the skills that
  were used

· Establish a real audience
· Share learners' efforts
· Make real use of learners'
  work
· Encourage a variety of
  communication strategies
· Encourage different
  learning/communicating styles

Learn from experience

Communicate

What have I learned?

Let's tell someone!

TA

Evaluate

How well did I do?

Let's do it!

Implement

· Encourages an approach
  of 'learning how to learn'
· Builds 'tools' for
  self-assessment
· Promotes learning as a
  growth process
· Establishes 'mistakes'
  as growth points
· Discourages 'right
  first time' approach

· Discuss whether the goal was
  achieved
· Check against criteria
· Consider ways to improve
· Target specific ways to
  improve
· Give opportunity for
  re-doing/improving
· Check on group/
  individual efficiency

· Use a variety of
  methods/formats
· Encourage a variety of
  activities
· Develop a repertoire of recording
  skills
· Teach/model an important
  procedure
· Check on progress

· Develops flexibility
· Uses a variety of activities
· Allows for different learning styles
· Encourages creativity
· Discourages 'templates' of one model/style
· Promotes a variety of responses

© Belle Wallace (2002) Teachers Problem-Solving and Thinking Skills across the Middle Year

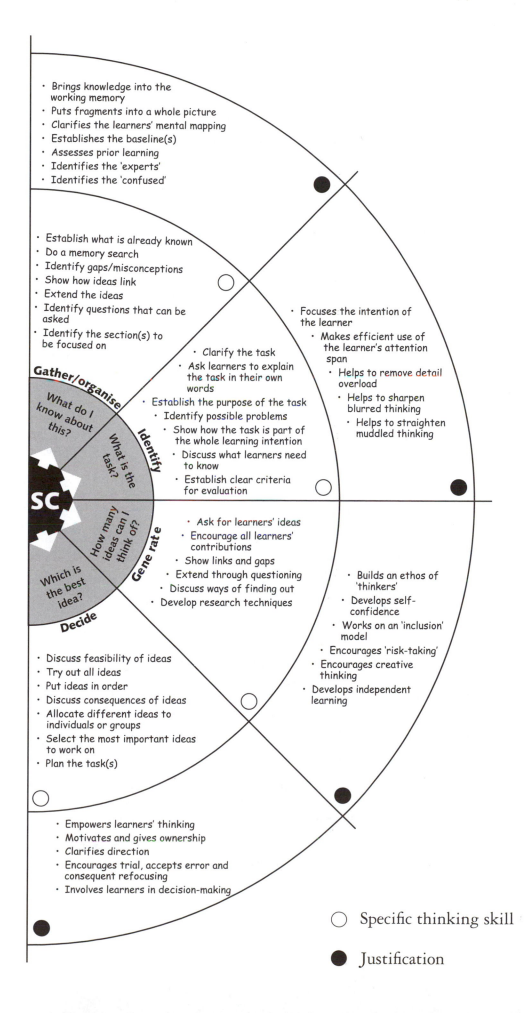

- Brings knowledge into the working memory
- Puts fragments into a whole picture
- Clarifies the learners' mental mapping
- Establishes the baseline(s)
- Assesses prior learning
- Identifies the 'experts'
- Identifies the 'confused'

- Establish what is already known
- Do a memory search
- Identify gaps/misconceptions
- Show how ideas link
- Extend the ideas
- Identify questions that can be asked
- Identify the section(s) to be focused on

Gather/organise

What do I know about this?

What is the task?

Identify

SC

How many ideas can I think of?

Generate

Which is the best idea?

Decide

- Clarify the task
- Ask learners to explain the task in their own words
- Establish the purpose of the task
- Identify possible problems
- Show how the task is part of the whole learning intention
- Discuss what learners need to know
- Establish clear criteria for evaluation

- Focuses the intention of the learner
- Makes efficient use of the learner's attention span
- Helps to remove detail overload
- Helps to sharpen blurred thinking
- Helps to straighten muddled thinking

- Ask for learners' ideas
- Encourage all learners' contributions
- Show links and gaps
- Extend through questioning
- Discuss ways of finding out
- Develop research techniques

- Builds an ethos of 'thinkers'
- Develops self-confidence
- Works on an 'inclusion' model
- Encourages 'risk-taking'
- Encourages creative thinking
- Develops independent learning

- Discuss feasibility of ideas
- Try out all ideas
- Put ideas in order
- Discuss consequences of ideas
- Allocate different ideas to individuals or groups
- Select the most important ideas to work on
- Plan the task(s)

- Empowers learners' thinking
- Motivates and gives ownership
- Clarifies direction
- Encourages trial, accepts error and consequent refocusing
- Involves learners in decision-making

○ Specific thinking skill

● Justification

Appendix 4

Basic and Advanced Thinking Skills and Strategies (Tools)

TASC	Gather and Organise	Identify	Generate	Decide
Key Questions	What do I already know about this? Make links and group ideas together. Maybe organise information as a mind map.	What are we trying to do? What are our success criteria? How will we know if we have done a good job? What do we need to do this?	How many ways can we do this? Who can we ask to help us? Where can we find out? Let's all think about this.	Which is the best way? What should we do first? Why should we do it this way? What will happen if we do this?
Advanced Thinking Skills	Searching memory; recalling from past experiences; recalling from recent stimuli; Hitch-hiking onto others' ideas; Organising links.	Clarifying goals; considering success criteria; consulting others.	Creating a 'think-tank'; considering end product and research possibilities; consulting others.	Looking at both sides of an idea; exploring the consequences; considering all factors; prioritising; hypothesising; predicting; consulting others.
Useful Strategies (Tools)	Ordering pictures; branch diagrams; mind mapping; bubble maps; deliberate mistakes; KWHL grids; follow-me cards; true or false cards; concept cartoons.	Think-Pair-Share; flowcharts; forcefield analysis; 'What? When? Where? Why? How?'	Thought showers; hitch-hiking; concept maps; creative connections; graphical metaphors; forced metaphors.	Think-Pair-Share; ranking charts; flowcharts; practical, not practical; SWOT Analysis.
Higher Order Thinking Skills	Organising; linking knowledge, senses and feelings.	Questioning; re-phrasing suggestions; initiating ideas.	Generating ideas; questioning; comparing and contrasting.	Reasoning; questioning; clarifying; disagreeing; justifying; revising ideas; decision-making; planning.
Repertoire of Basic Thinking Skills	*These basic thinking skills need to be taught, practised and developed and form the basic* verbs, adverbs, nouns, adjectives in different contexts across the curriculum. communication and recording skills. Rich repertoire of varied sensory experiential			

The extended TASC process showing how sections of the TASC Problem-solving Processes blend into a coherent whole

Implement	Evaluate	Communicate	Learn from Experience
Is our plan working? Should we change anything? What do we do next?	Are we pleased with this? Have we done it well? Have we achieved our success criteria? How could we do it better?	Who can we tell about this? How can we show other people? How can we explain? How can we make it interesting?	What have we learned to do? How else can we use this? How do we feel now? What are we proud of?
Interpreting; applying; creating; designing; investigating; composing; consulting others.	Observing, interacting and responding to others; appraising process and product; consulting others.	Presenting; demonstrating; explaining; clarifying; justifying; consulting others.	Reflecting; making connections; transferring across the curriculum; crystallising; consolidating; extending.
Think-Pair-Share; planning grids; flowcharts; sketches.	Think-Pair-Share; extend Mindmaps; 3 Stars and a wish; next steps.	Recording across the multiple abilities: displays, performances, visuals, structures, role-plays, recordings, video clips, games.	Think-Pair-Share; extend Mindmaps; 3 Stars and a wish; consequences.
Organising; reviewing; monitoring; questioning; re-thinking Developing ideas; adapting.	Evaluating; questioning; assessing; judging.	Summarising; sharing; expressing ideas and opinions.	Reflecting; generalising; summarising.

building blocks for thinking and problem-solving. Appropriate, fluent use of prepositions, conjunctions, Appropriate use of basic concepts in number, measures, shape, space. Appropriate use of basic learning